Learning to Read for Teens
A Remedial Program for the Teenage Student

Daniel Langer
3333 Henry Hudson Parkway, 17M
Bronx, New York 10463
Dan7L.dan@gmail.com

Revised Edition, 2019
© Daniel Langer March, 2019
© Copyright by Daniel Langer, January 16, 1996, under title:
Spelling to Read For Teens: A Linguistic Reading Program
Library of Congress #TXu 721-012
KDP ISBN 9781090806024

All rights reserved.
No part of this book may be reproduced or utilized in any form or by any mechanical or electronic means, including photocopying without written or email permission from the author.
Dan7L.dan@gmail.com

TABLE OF CONTENTS

Teacher's Guide   6

WORD LIST 1: Can the Man Rap?   9
Skills: (short a and i)

WORD LIST 2: The Picnic   12
Skills: Plural 's', possessive 's', s=/s/, s=/z/, two syllable words (short 'a' and 'i'), blends.

WORD LIST 3: He Said She Said   15
Skills: (-ing), (-ink), (-ill),(-int),(-mp),(-nd)

WORD LIST 4: Playing the Sax for Six Days   18
Skills: (-x=/ks/, sk, -ve, [No English word ends with v: a silent e is added.]

WORD LIST 5: Stranded for Six Days   20
Skills: 5 [*past time* suffix, "ed"]
(-ed=/t/, when added to words *not* ending in "t'or "d", as in washed, asked, mixed.)
(-ed=/id/ when added to a word ending in "t" or "d", as in handed, printed.)

WORD LIST 6: Stickball   22
Skills: (-ll), (-ff), (-ss), (-ck) (-zz).
SPELLING RULE: In one syllable words that have a short vowel,
double the final s, f, l, or z. (Exceptions: if, is, his, has, was, gas, this).

WORD LIST 7: Nuts About You!   25
Skills: (short u, multisyllabic words)

WORD LIST 8: The Football Game   29
Skills: (sh), (ch),(-tch = /ch/), (qu = /kw/)
Spelling rule: The sound /ch/ is spelled 'ch' or 'tch'. The short vowel needs an extra letter 't' (witch). If the short vowel already has consonant after it, do not add the 't' (pinch).

WORD LIST 9: In Handcuffs   33
   Skills: (th [the], (th [thin], (compound words)

WORD LIST 10;DISCO   36
Skills: Open Syllable at end of a word), (-y = long /i/)

WORD LIST 11: Shake to the Disco!   39
SKILLS: (Silent e: a-e)

WORD LIST 12: A Dive in the Lake   42
SKILLS: (i-e)

WORD LIST 13: Excuse Me!   46
SKILLS: (u-e)

WORD LIST14 : Locked Up by a Cop   48
SKILLS: (short 'o')

WORD LIST 15 : Without a Rope   52
SKILLS: (o-e)

WORD LIST 16: Midnight in a Cave   56
SKILLS: (igh=long *i*)

WORD LIST 17: This is the End!   60
SKILLS: (short e)

WORD LIST 18: Pete's Rice and Beans   65
SKILLS: (e-e)

WORD LIST 19: The Herb   68
SKILLS: (-er)

WORD LIST 20: I've Had it Up to Here!   70
SKILLS: (contractions)

WORD LIST 21: A Kiss He Will Never Forget   72
SKILLS: (ar,or)

WORD LIST 22: Submerged in Water   75
SKILLS: (er, ir, ur)

WORD LIST 23: Action in a Crisis   79
SKILLS: (Open and closed syllables, -tion)

WORD LIST 24: Jail Years   81
SKILLS: (ee, ea, ai, -ought)

WORD LIST 25: A Prayer and a Groan   85
SKILLS: (ay, oa)

WORD LIST 26: Body on Ice   89
SKILLS: (-y = long /e/, suffix -ly)

WORD LIST 27: A Mouse in the House   94
SKILLS: (-old, -ild, -ind, ou, ow = /ou/ or /long o/)

WORD LIST 28: Busboy at a Restaurant   100
SKILLS: (-oy, -oi, -aw, -au, c=/s/)

WORD LIST 29: Nat's New Rap Song   104
SKILLS: (-ong, -ung, -unk)

WORD LIST 30: The Agreement   106
SKILLS: (suffixes: es, est, ful, less, ment, ness, en=/in/)

WORD LIST 31: Smoking Jill   109
SKILLS: (Silent 'e', doubling consonant rule)

WORD LIST 32: Good Snaps, Poor Snaps   112
SKILLS: (oo, oo, ou, ui)

WORD LIST 33: A Trophy for the Dumbest Snap   115
SKILLS: (Silent letters, ph=/f/)

WORD LIST 34: Feeling Miserable   **117**
SKILLS: (-le)

WORD LIST 35: Chance at Magic   **120**
SKILLS: (c=/s/, g=/j/)

WORD LIST 36: Especially for You   **123**
SKILLS: (suffixes: ous, ture; ci and ti = /sh/, -sion)

Learning to Read for Teens
A Remedial Program for the Teenage Student

Teacher's Guide

This program is designed to meet the needs of learning disabled teenagers who have not mastered decoding skills. The program will work best with teens who are on a low second to fourth grade reading level. The program assumes that the student already knows most initial and final consonants, and some sight words. This is a typical profile for learning disabled middle school students. The pace of the program is geared for the older student (middle school or high school), and the stories are of high interest, involving problems that are often encountered by inner city adolescents. The sequence of spelling/decoding skills include some more challenging skills early on to meet the needs of the student having better skills.

The stories run like a novel, with character development and problems that continue from one chapter to the next. The classroom teacher or parent should guide discussions before and after each reading pertinent to the story. Some of the topics that are reflected in the stories are: humor, instigating arguments, dealing with insults, fighting and how to avoid fighting, sports, boyfriend/girlfriend relationships, hazards of smoking, danger of drinking and driving, dealing with anger, snapping on friends, crime, prison, abusive parents and spouses, loyalty, love, when bad things happen to good people, and long range life goals.

Before reading a story, students are taught to spell and to read words from a word list. The words are in linguistic patterns. If a student can spell a word, he will be able to read the word. *For Reading Only* word lists often follow the regular word list. These words are frequently sight words, but they also include other words that will appear in other lists later on. Words in the *For Reading Only* lists were added to allow the reading passages to flow like ordinary speaking patterns. *All the words in a given story come from the current word list or a previous word list.*

Students beginning the program should already be familiar with most of the *For Reading Only* words on the first list. If the first lists are very difficult for a particular student, it may be necessary to do other remediation on consonant sounds and basic sight words before beginning the program. If the student finds the words in early word lists to be too easy, the student should just read the stories until he or she gets up to more challenging word lists for spelling and reading. On the other hand, if a student can read and *spell* all the words on the last few lists, he/she should be given other vocabulary and reading material. However, that student may still benefit from comprehension of stories and discussion of themes. Many of the stories end with cliff hangers, as in a soap opera, and students are anxious to keep reading to see what will happen next.

If a particular class is too advanced for the beginning word lists, they should read the stories from the beginning relatively quickly for the purpose of becoming familiar with the characters and their particular problems. References to events in the first story are made in the last story.

Very often, a given classroom has students at different levels. The word lists are designed to meet the needs of students with varying decoding and spelling skills. Words pertaining to the new spelling/reading skills appear in the left columns and uppermost rows. Words on the bottom rows are more difficult than those at the top, often using phonemes from previous lessons. The right column often has more difficult words, but it only uses sounds and syllables that have been introduced in the current or in a previous lesson.

Cooperative learning techniques can be very useful. Students should test each other in small groups for spelling and reading on each word list. The groups need not be homogeneous. More advanced students can help weaker students. Peer teaching can sharpen the spelling and decoding skills of the more advanced student. Students should also practice reading the stories orally to each other. The teacher should give the students practice by frequent dictations. Before beginning a new word list, the teacher should give a spelling test from the current word list.

Each weekly lesson should include the following elements:

1. Review of previous lessons in spelling and reading.
2. Introduce new word patterns. Use minimal contrast wherever possible.
For example, in word list #7, the students can copy h_t, h_t, h_t from the board, and the teacher can dictate the words *hat, hit, hut,* asking the student to write the missing vowel. Then they should read the three words out loud. The same can be done for *fan, fin, fun,* asking the students to fill in the missing *a, i,* or *u.* Then the teacher can erase the words from the board and dictate whole words for the students to write.
3. Dictate most of the basic words from the word list. Include dictation of sentences.
4. Give out word lists, and have students read out loud from the lists. More advanced readers can be challenged with words from the right column and bottom rows. Students who are struggling can be asked to read the basic words for the new decoding skill from the left columns and top rows. If the students find the early lists easy to read, they can skip the spelling exercises until they reach a level that is challenging.
5. After some practice, introduce and distribute the new story for the list. The stories should be read out loud by students in the class. The teacher can model oral reading by reading parts of the story to the class. After discussion, the students should break up into groups of two to four and practice reading out loud to each other. Silent reading should also be encouraged.
6. Students should be given written assignments based on the stories. Students should be asked to use words from the lists in sentences. They can make separate lists of their own of nouns, verbs, etc., using words from the list. They can be asked to find the word in column x that means so and so, or the opposite of so and so. Parents should be encouraged to have their child practice reading and spelling each word list and story. Reinforcement is very important.
6. After studying in groups and individually, students should be given a spelling test with selected words from the list, followed by an individualized oral reading test with about

10—20 words. The teacher should select the appropriate rows and columns to match each student's skills.

The program can be taught in one year or less, leaving each student with spelling and decoding skills for most of the phonemes in the English language. Total reading comprehension should also show significant improvement. Learning disabled teens reading on a second to fourth grade reading level will experience the thrill of being able to read a book that was not made for little kids.[1]

---

[1] There is a follow-up reader with more advanced word lists, incorporating the same characters with science content for teens reading at a fourth to sixth grade reading level – The Cool Science Reader: A Remedial Reading and Science Program for the Teenage Student.

WORD LIST 1 (short a and i)
Read down each column. If you can spell these words, yo can read them.

at	it	man
sat	sit	ran
hat	hit	can
bat	bit	pan
fat	pit	Ann
rat	spit	and
mat	with	hand
Nat	will	mad
cat	in	sad
scat	if	bad
that	is	had
tap	his	bag
rap	has	big
nap	hid	kiss
cap	did	this
lap	lip	am
clap	Tim	champ

WORD LIST # 1B

For Reading Only

into	with	took
were	the	street
you	to	I
said	good	go
a	little	was
your	do	not
on	my	saw
for	this	have
no		

Word List 1 (Short 'a', short 'i')

Can the Man Rap?

Ann, Nat, and Tim were in the street.
"Can you rap?" Ann said to Nat.
"Can I rap?" said Nat.
"That is what I said," said Ann. "Can you rap?"
"I can rap good!" said Nat. "Can you clap?"
Ann said, "If you can rap, I can clap."
"Go clap, and I will rap," said Nat.
Ann sat and did a little clap.
Nat said, "That clap was a little tap. I said *clap*!"
Ann did a big clap.
Nat said to Tim, "Ann can clap to the rap. Can you tap your lip and spit to the rap?"
"I can tap my lip to the rap," said Tim. "I am a champ!"
Ann said, "I can clap with my hand, and Tim can spit and tap his lip. Tim has a good lip to tap and spit to the rap. If Nat can do a rap, he can have a **kiss**."
Nat said, "I am the man! I can rap! I am a champ at rap! I can rap for a **kiss**!" Nat did this rap:

A big fat man had a big fat hat.
His big fat cat took a nap on the cap.
The big fat man said to his cat,
"Scat, cat, do not sit on my cap!"
The cat was sad, and he sat on a mat.
A big fat rat sat on the mat.
The cat ran to the man and sat on his lap.
The big fat man was mad at his cat.
He took the cat and hit him with a rag.
The cat ran to the mat, and the man saw the rat.
"Scat, rat," the man said to the rat.
The rat ran to the cap and hid in the hat.
The fat man ran and took a big fat pan.
He hit the pan with a big fat bat.
The big fat rat ran into the cat.
The cat hit and bit that big fat rat.
The cat, you see, was a fat, fat cat!

Ann said, "Nat, that rap was bad! It was not fat. You are not a champ at rap. No kiss for you!"

WORD LIST 2
(Plural 's', possessive 's', s=/s/, s=/z/, two syllable words (short 'a' and 'i'), blends.)
Read down and across. If you can spell these words, you can read them.

cats	as	sip	park
rats	has	rip	parks
hats	cans	trip	milk
bats	fans	trips	sits
mats	bags	lips	hits
map	tags	slips	fits
maps	flags	clips	zig zag
naps	glad	ants	pic nic
caps	crabs	pants	cab in
claps	pans	plant	lim it
slaps	plans	plants	fin ish
Sam	hands	taps	pan ic
lamp	stands	trap	vic tim
lamps	Ann's	traps	van ish
champs	man's	snap	ba na na
split	Sam's	snaps	ba na nas

For Reading Only

they	he	want	we
her	be	of	she
are	see	know	sees
friend	comes	girlfriend	look
hello	says	who	Hector
out	Hector's	going	singing
there	were		

Word List 2 (plural 's', consonant blends)

The Picnic

Hector and Ann are going on a picnic. Ann and Hector have 2 hats and 2 picnic bags. The trip to the park is zigzag. Hector has to look at a map. In the park, Hector and Ann see a cabin. There are 2 flags on the cabin. It is the park man's cabin.

Ann says, "I want to go in." Hector and Ann tap on the cabin as they go in. They see 4 plants, 3 mats, 9 stamps, 1 bag of clips, 2 fans, 6 cans, 5 pans, 2 maps, 3 bats, 2 rats, 4 rat traps, and 3 lamps. Hector says, "Ann, clap your hands." Ann claps her hands and the lamps go on. Hector sees a big fat cat on a mat. Ann sees bananas on a mat and crabs in a pan. The park man did not finish his crabs. No man is in the cabin. Did the park man vanish?

Hector stands on the mat. He did not see the bananas on the mat. Hector trips on a banana, and he hits the fat cat. The cat is mad. The cat sits on Hector's cap. Hector has 2 rips in his pants, and he is sad.

Ann sees a man going to the cabin. It is the park man. "We are in the park man's cabin!" Ann says. "It is bad to be in the park man's cabin. The park man will be mad. He will hit me in the lip! I do not want to be a victim of a split lip."

"He will not hit you in the lip. He will not be mad. Do not panic. I know the park man. Sam, the park man, will be glad to see me. He is my friend. You will not be a victim of a split lip."

The park man comes into the cabin. "Hello, Hector," says Sam. "I am glad to see you. Who is your friend?"

"Sam," says Hector. "This is Ann, my girlfriend. Ann, this is Sam, the park man."

"Hello, Sam," says Ann. "This cabin is fat!"

"Hello, Ann," says Sam. "Do you want a sip of milk?"

"No," says Ann. "Hector and I are going on a picnic."

"I am glad," says Sam. "It is good to go on a picnic!"

Hector and Ann go out of Sam's cabin. Ann taps Hector on the hand as she says to Hector, "I did not know I was your girlfriend!"

"Are you mad?" says Hector.

"No," says Ann. "I am glad!"

Illustration by Jenna Ellison

Hector and Ann go hand in hand to the picnic.

WORD LIST 3a (-ing), (-ink), (-ill), (-int), (-mp), (-nd)
Read down and across. . If you can spell these words, you can read them.

king	fish	ink	lamp
ring	dish	sink	damp
rings	wish	stink	camp
ring ing	wish ing	stinks	stamp
sing	fish ing	stink ing	camp ing
sings	fast	think	ant
sing ing	last	drink	plant
wing	last ing	think ing	plant ing
swing	list	lift	land
swings	will	lift ing	band
swing ing	kill	print ing	wind
thing	hill	sprint ing	hand ing
sting	pill	him	stand ing
stings	spill	limp	hand bag
sting ing	still	limp ing	Hand stand
string	will ing		out stand ing

WORD LIST 3b

<u>For Reading Only</u>

kissing	up	by	kick
because	talk	gave	about
but	being	kick	now
them	even	about	start
then	never	now	kidding
when	very	start	so
what	why	kidding	or
told	would	so	kick
say	love	or	about
saying	came	by	now
foot	some	gave	start
kidding	so	or	

Word List 3 (-ing), (-ink), (-ill), (-int), (-mp)

He Said She Said

Tim was standing in the street. Tim saw Nat limping, and Tim said to Nat, "That is a bad limp. Why are you limping?"

Nat said, "Why am I *limping*? I am limping because of *you*! I want to hit you in the lip!"

Tim said, "Look, man, if you start swinging at me I will start swinging at you. If I hit you, you will wish you were still limping, because you will not be standing!"

Nat was mad. He was lifting his hand to hit Tim, when he saw Ann sprinting fast up the street.

She ran over to them and said, "Why do you look so mad?"

Nat said to Ann, "Tim told Hector that you said that you would kiss me for some good rap singing."

"Your rap singing stinks," Ann said to Nat. "I would never kiss you! I was kidding when I said I would kiss you for your rap singing. Tim, what did you say to Hector?"

"I told him that you love Nat's rap singing and that Nat is thinking of kissing you."

"Tim, I am very mad at you for saying that," said Ann. "Nat, what did Hector say to you when he saw you?"

"Hector said that Tim said that I was thinking of kissing you, and that I was wishing you were my girlfriend," said Nat.

"Then Hector said to me, 'You think that by rap singing, Ann will kiss you on the lips?!'

"I said, 'I am a champ at rap singing....' Then Hector gave me a rap in the lip and a kick on the foot. My lip is still stinging, and I am limping on my foot. He hit me because of what Tim said! That is why I am mad at Tim. I have a big lip because Tim has a big trap!"

Then Hector came sprinting up the street. He ran up to Nat and said, "Not so fast, Nat. If you are still wishing to kiss Ann, then that will be your last wish, you stinking fish!"

"Do not hit Nat!" said Ann. "Why are you so mad at him?"

Hector said, "Tim said that you said...."

"You hit Nat because of *he said that she said*?" said Ann. "Did you talk to me or to Nat? *No!* I was not wishing to kiss Nat or thinking about being his girlfriend! I was thinking about kissing *you*, Hector, but not now!" Then Ann hit Hector with her handbag. She did not even look at Tim.

WORD LIST 4 (-x=/ks/, sk, -ve, [No English word ends with v; a silent e is added])
Read down and across. If you can spell these words, you can read them.

ax	kid	have
tax	kids	give
wax	skid	live
fax	skit	cap tive
sax	skin	ac tive
lax	skip	in ac tive
six	risk	vin dic tive
fix	ask	ask ing
mix	mask	tax ing
lit	task	wax ing
slit	fix ing	mix ing

For Reading Only

fun	asked	doing	room
floor	playing	days	day
mother	cannot	sorry	wants
house	put	where	

Word List 4 (-x), (sk), (-ve)

Playing the Sax for Six Days

Hector was in his house with his mother. His mother was waxing the floor. Waxing the floor was a very taxing task. Hector had a split in the skin of his hand, and he was fixing his hand.

Hector's mother said, "What are you doing with your hand?"

"The skin on my hand is split, and I am fixing it," said Hector.

"Why is your skin split?" asked Mother. "Who slit your skin?"

"I was playing with Nat and his lip hit my hand."

"Are you saying that the kid's lip hit your hand?"

"Yes, Mother," said Hector. "Nat has a very active lip!"

"Do not play with me! Nat's lip did not hit your hand. You hit Nat!" Hector's mother was very mad. "Why did you hit him?!"

"I hit Nat because Tim said that Nat said that he wants to kiss Ann," said Hector.

"I am going to fix you, Hector!" his mother said. "You do not have to hit Nat because of *he said she said* . You took a big risk when you hit Nat in the lip. Nat has a friend who is a champ at hitting kids. His friend can be very vindictive. If his friend hits you, he can kill you! He can slit you with an ax. I do not want you hitting your friends!"

"I am sorry, Mother," said Hector. "I have to go out, now."

"Where do you think you are going?" asked Mother.

"Out to see Ann."

"You are not going out," said Mother. "You are not going to see Ann. You will have to live in your room for six days!"

"I have to be captive in my room for *six days*?" asked Hector. "What am I going to do in my room for six days? I want to be active! If I have to be in my room for six days, then I will be inactive. Being inactive is not good for me. You do not want to be vindictive, Mother, do you? Can I sit in my room for 2 days, and then go out?"

"Sorry, Hector," said Mother. "I said six days! I am not being vindictive. It is not good for a mother to be lax with her kids. I am asking you not to hit your friends. I will give you a mask. You can put on a mask and do a skit. Doing a skit can be fun."

"I have to have six kids to do a good skit," said Hector.

"You cannot see your friends for six days. You can play your sax in your room. In six days, you will be very good at playing the sax. You can be in the band. If you want to talk to Ann, you can print what you want to say and fax it to her."

WORD LIST 5 [*past time* suffix, "ed"]
 (-ed=/id/ when added to a word ending in "t" or "d", as in handed, printed.)
 (-ed=/t/, when added to words *not* ending in "t'or "d", as in washed, asked, mixed.)

hand	mix	washed
handed	mix ing	wash ing
landed	mixed	cashed
last	fixed	crashed
lasted	waxed	mashed
print ing	taxed	smashed
printed	risked	smash ing
planted	asked	flash
lift	fish ing	flashed
lifted	fished	slanted
drifted	wished	twisted
tilted	past	stranded
wilted	stand	fin ished

For Reading Only

would	looked	from	killing
could	talked	OK	stick
should	played	TV	snack
water	slipped	only	food
cannot	wanted	went	

Word List 5 (-ed)

Stranded for Six Days

Hector's mother said that he had to be in his room for six days. He could not go out to see Ann or his friends. All that Hector could do was look at TV and play his Sax. He looked at TV. He played his sax. He looked at TV. He washed and waxed his sax. He looked at TV.

Hector said, "I cannot stand it! I am stranded in my room for six days! I want to smash the TV and smash my sax. I have to go out! I am asking you, mother, can I go out now?"

"Sorry, Hector," said Mother. "You can go out when the six days are finished. I do not want you lifting your hands to hit Nat. I do not want you smashing your friend's lips!" Hector's mother handed Hector a snack of mashed bananas.

"Mashed bananas?" asked Hector. "This food is killing me."

Hector washed his hands and mixed the mashed bananas, but the bananas did not go past his lips. Hector wished he could go out. He wished he had not smashed Nat's lip. "Ann did not want to kiss Nat," Hector said. "She said she wanted to kiss *me* ! I should have talked to Ann and Nat. I should not have hit my friend because of *he said she said* ."

Mother said, "I am glad you said that. You can go fishing with your friends in six days."

Mother lifted a plant from the floor. She said, "Ann planted this plant. She gave me the plant to give to you. She said she wanted you to think of her when you look at the plant." Mother handed the plant to Hector.

Hector did not water the plant. In 3 days the plant was tilted. In six days the plant was wilted. Hector slipped, and the plant crashed to the floor. The plant was twisted. Hector could not fix the plant. Ann's plant lasted six days with Hector.

The six days were finished. Hector went fishing with Nat and Tim. Hector said to Nat, "I am sorry I smashed your lip. My hand slipped."

"That's OK," said Nat. "My lip is fixed, now." Nat hit Hector's fishing stick. The stick slipped from Hector's hand and in the water.

"Sorry, Hector," said Nat. "My hand slipped."

Hector's fishing stick drifted in the water. The stick landed in the sand. Hector looked mad. Nat took the stick and gave it to Hector. "I was only kidding," said Nat. "You should be glad I washed your stick."

WORD LIST 6 (-ll), (-ff), (-ss), (-ck) (-zz)
SPELLING RULE: In one syllable words that have a short vowel, double the final *s, f, l,* or *z*. (Exceptions: *if, is, his, has, was, gas, this*).

all	kiss	if	sack	packed
ball	kissed	stiff	rack	lacks
call	miss	staff	pack	licked
fall	missed	sniff	lack	picked
Bill	miss ing	sniffed	lick	kicked
Jill	pass	cliff	pick	sniffed
will	passed	jazz	kick ing	slick
wall	pass ing	fizz	back	slacks
hill	hiss	Jack	black	stickball
hall	hissed	sack	snack	smack
ill	mass	sick	track	smacked
pill	class	tick	crack	snacked
spill	glass	kick	stack	cracked
still	grass	brick	stick	called
skill	blast	strict	trick	
grill	bliss			

For Reading Only

like	trapped	tapped	sitting
way	tripped	thanks	thank
too	winning	please	kidding
door	flipped	again	kidded

I'll = I will

Word List 6 (-ss, ff, ll, zz, ck)

Stickball

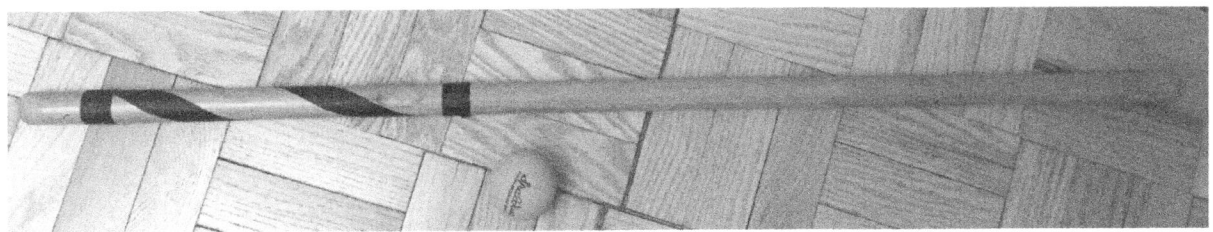

Hector, Tim, Ann, Nat, Jack, Jill and Bill were playing stickball in the park. Hector was at bat. Hector missed the ball — 1 out. Jill hissed at Hector.

"You stink, Hector," kidded Ann. "You missed the ball."

Jack was at bat. He picked up a black stickball bat and tapped it on the grass. He licked his lips. Then Jack smacked the ball. The ball went to the wall. Jack ran on all the bags. Jack's kids were winning.

"What a blast!" said Ann. "You smacked that ball good!"

"I do not lack the skill to hit a ball," said Jack. "I am a champ at stickball!"

Bill was at bat. Bill hit the ball to the wall. Tim ran back on the grass to the wall. Ann saw the ball fall in Tim's hands. Bill was out.

Ann was at bat. "Do not play back — come all the way in!" called Jack. "She cannot hit the ball."

Ann hit the ball to Nat. Nat missed the ball. The ball passed Nat. Ann is a track champ, and she ran fast. Ann was on the bag. Hector was at bat, again.

Jack said, "You do not have to go back for Hector. You do not have to come in. You can sit on the grass. The ball will not pass you because Hector lacks the skill to hit a ball. Hector stinks at stickball."

Hector took the bat and ran at Jack. "You say I do not have the skill to hit a ball, but I do have the skill to crack this stick on your big, fat lip! You think you are slick, but I'll hit you with a brick. I will kick you in the foot, and then you will be limping when you go out to play ball."

"You call this playing ball?" asked Nat. "I do not like all this jazz about hitting kids in the lip and kicking them in the foot. You said you were sorry for smacking me in the lip and kicking me in the foot. I was limping for six days. Now you want to crack the stickball bat on Jack!"

Hector said, "I was sad when Ann said that I stink. I was mad when Ann said that Jack smacked the ball good. I wanted to pack my bag and go back to my house and play the sax. When Jack said all this jazz about sitting down when I was at bat, I cracked."

Jack said, "Go play your sax, Hector! You stink at stickball!"

Hector cracked the black stickball bat on a picnic grill. He bit his lip, and he kicked the grass, but he did not hit Jack. Hector did not want to be in his room for six days again.

Ann was very glad that Hector did not hit Jack. She was very mad at Jack for picking on Hector. "You have no class!" Ann said to Jack. "The things you said to Hector are sick. You can hit the ball, but you are not a hit with your friends. You should not say bad things to your friends. Go play on a cliff!"

Nat did this rap:

"Jack hit the ball to the wall,
and he ran on all the bags.
But when Jack tripped on his big fat lip,
he had a big fat fall."

Ann looked at Jack and said, "Now, say you are sorry."

"Sorry," sniffed Jack. "I am licked." Jack packed his ball and bag and went back to his house.

"I did it again," said Hector. "I was mad, and I wanted to smack Jack. Why do I want to hit my friends when I am mad?"

"The trick," said Ann, "is not to be so mad because of the sick things that some kids say."

Hector said, "I was sad when you said that I stink because I missed the ball and was called out, but I know you were only kidding. When Jill hissed at me, I was a little mad. Then Jack snapped at me and I flipped. I was so mad that I wanted to kick Jack's foot and smack his fat lip. I have to talk to Sam, the park man. Please come with me to his cabin, Ann."

"OK," said Ann.

Ann and Hector went up the hill to the park man's cabin. Hector tapped on the door.

Sam, the park man, went to the door, and he said, "Come in, Hector. Come in Ann. Please, sit down. Do you wish to have a snack?"

"No thank you," said Hector. "I have to talk to you. When I was mad at Nat, I hit him in the lip and kicked him in the foot. Nat's lip was stinging, and he was limping on his foot for six days. I was stranded in my room for six days, and I could not go out to see Ann. Now I am mad at Jack, and I want to smack him in the lip. When I am mad, I want to hit my friends. I do not know why. Why do I have to hit and kick when I am mad?"

"I think I know why," said Sam. "When you were little, your dad would hit you when he was mad. He hit your mother, too. Your mother does not want you to be like your dad. That is why she is so strict with you. That is why you had to be in your room for six days. You want to hit back at your dad, but you cannot. Your dad split. He ran out on you and your mother. You cannot hit back at your dad by hitting your friends."

"Thanks, Sam," said Hector. "I will have to think about what you said."

WORD LIST 7a (Short *u*).

up	run	mud	puff
cup	fun	must	huff
pup	gun	just	cuff
us	sun	gust	stuff
pus	bun	dust	bucks
bus	hunt	trust	suck
cut	grunt	crust	duck
but	hum	suds	puck
nut	gum	mugs	luck
shut	glum	sulk	truck
slut	plum	in sult	stuck
mug	plump	jump ing	shucks
hug	jump	jumped	ducked
rug	lump	bumped	stump
bug	dump	bump ing	slumped
dug	bump		

WORD LIST 7b (Short *u*, multisyllabic words
If you can spell the word list, you can read them.)

cat	fun	rub	pub lic
cut	him	rib	hus band
hit	ham	hunt	grunt ed
hat	hum	hint	nap kin
hut	ran	bad	pump kin
but	run	sad	huff ing
bat	must	suds	puff ing
bit	mist	nuts	dis rupt
big	truck	sack	dis rupt ing
bag	trick	sick	in sult
bug	lick	suck ing	in sult ing

For Reading Only

walk	act	giving	cuff
walked	eye	rubbing	rubbed
walking	eyes	running	stubbed
tree	Oh	acting	slapped
having	get	hugged	started
don't	after	kind	I'm = I am

Word List 7 (short *u*)

Nuts About You!

Hector and Ann went back to the park. The sun was out, but there was a big wind. A gust of wind hit Hector's cap. His hat was on the grass, and some dust went into his eye. Hector rubbed his eye with a rag.

"Don't rub your eye with a rag, Hector," said Ann. "Rubbing your eye with a rag can give you a sick eye. You could get pus in your eye. You must have some water and some suds."

"We can get a bit of water at the snack truck," said Hector.

Hector looked at Ann run to the snack truck. The man in the snack truck handed Ann a cup of water and a napkin. Ann put the napkin in the cup of water, and she ran back to Hector. Ann took the napkin out of the cup of water, and she rubbed the napkin on Hector's eye. The dust came out of Hector's eye. Hector was glad. Ann gave Hector a hug and a little kiss on his eye. Now Hector was *very* glad! Hector started to hum and sing. Then he started running and jumping up and down. Hector was acting like a ham.

"Hector," said Ann." I know you are glad that I gave you a hug and a kiss, but you are acting like a nut!"

"I was only kidding," said Hector, "but that was some hug! And what a kiss!"

"Hector, you are a nut, but I like nuts."

"You like nuts?" asked Hector. "Would you like to have a nut bun for a snack? I have six bucks."

Hector and Ann went back to the snack truck. Hector gave the man 2 bucks for a nut bun, 2 mugs of milk, and 2 plums. Hector cut the bun and gave some of the bun to Ann with a mug of milk and a plum.

"Thank you, Hector, but you don't have to suck up to me by giving me a nut bun, a mug of milk, and a plum for a hug and a kiss," kidded Ann. "Do you think I am some kind of slut that you have to give me food for a kiss?"

"I am not sucking up to you," said Hector. "I was just thinking that you would like a snack and a drink. Don't you trust me?"

"I trust you the way I would trust a man who gave me a nut bun on a public bus," kidded Ann. "It is no fun to kiss you. Kissing you is like kissing a rug with dust and crust. Would you like some gum? I am giving you a hint. If you want a kiss, get some gum!"

"Don't insult me like that!" said Hector. "I am not your husband!" Hector looked like a sad little pup. A mist came into his eyes, and he slumped down on the grass. He looked like a sulking lump of mud on the grass.

"Don't sulk," said Ann, sitting down on the grass. "I was only kidding."

"Don't kid like that," said Hector. "I don't like to be insulted."

"Insulting you is fun," said Ann. "It is fun to snap on you. You know that I was only kidding."

"I do not want to disrupt your fun, but it was not fun for me. I did not know you were kidding. I was thinking that you wanted to dump me."

"Oh, no," said Ann. "I don't want to dump you. You must know by now that I am stuck on you." Ann gave Hector a hug.

Hector said, "Come here my little pumpkin." Hector wanted to give Ann a kiss.

"Pumpkin?" asked Ann, disrupting Hector's kiss.

"Yes," kidded Hector. "You are a little plump like a pumpkin."

"You think I'm fat?"

"Oh no," kidded Hector. "You are not fat. You are not plump. You just look like a **pumpkin**!" Ann looked like a sad little pup. A mist came into her eyes. She slumped down on the grass and looked very glum. Hector gave Ann a hug. "Don't sulk," he said. "I was playing a trick on you. You know I was only kidding."

Ann slapped Hector with a rag, and hit him in the rib with her handbag. "Sorry Hector," she said. "I was only kidding!"

"Only kidding?" said Hector. Hector picked up a bug from the grass. "I will hit you with this bug**!**" he said. Ann ducked, and Hector missed hitting Ann with the bug. Hector picked up a bug from a tree trunk. Ann jumped up and ran. Hector ran after Ann. Ann was running fast. She ran past a hut in the park.

"You cannot hit me with that bug," called Ann. "You run like a duck! I am too fast for you! I am a champ at track."

Ann and Hector were having fun. The sun was out. Hector was huffing and puffing. He bumped into a tree stump and stubbed his foot.

"Don't trip on the tree stump!" called Ann. Hector did not trip on the tree stump, but he did slip on the mud. Hector had mud on the cuff of his pants.

"Don't fall!" called Ann. Hector looked up at Ann and slipped and tripped. Hector was down in the mud.

Ann walked back to Hector. "You are in luck, Hector," said Ann. "Little plump pigs like you love to play in the mud."

"And this little pig likes plump **pumpkins**," Hector said as he bumped into Ann.

"Don't bump into me!" said Ann.

Hector hugged Ann, and he licked her hand. "Sorry" grunted Hector, who was now acting like a pig. "This little pig likes to hunt for plump pumpkins."

"Shut up, Hector! Don't act like a ham!" said Ann. "If you bump me, lick me, or grunt at me again, I will smack you in the lip. Your lip will have a big lump."

"OK," said Hector. "I was just kidding. We were having fun."

"I know," said Ann. "I was kidding, too. I don't want you to have a lump on your lip when I kiss you."

"How about a kiss now?" asked Hector.

"Not now," kidded Ann. "I don't have any gum to give you."

"Oh, shucks!" said Hector.

Ann had black mud on her hands and on her slacks. "My mother will be mad at us when she sees all this mud on me, but we had fun!" said Ann. "We must be nuts!"

We are not nuts," said Hector. "It's just that I'm nuts about you!"

"And I am nuts about you, too!" said Ann.

Ann and Hector walked hand in hand to the bus.

WORD LIST 8 (sh), (ch), (-tch = /ch/), (qu = /kw/).
Spelling rule: The sound /ch/ is spelled 'ch' or 'tch'. The short vowel needs an extra letter 't' (witch). If the short vowel already has consonant after it, do not add the 't' (pinch).

ship	chip	chips	quit
shin	chick	chicks	quiz
cash	chin	itch	quick
mash	chat	ditch	quack
rash	chill	pitch	quilt
gash	champ	witch	quick sand
flash	chimp	switch	munched
trash	chump	switched	punched
smash	inch	stitch	pinched
crash	pinch	snitch	punch ing
crush	punch	snatch	chilled
rush	bunch	catch	chicks
hush	hunch	match	trash ing
blush	lunch	patch	watch
brushed	munch	batch	watch ing
Shift	much	clutch	tricked
fist	such	shrimp	sacked
cub	Cubs	branch	grand stand

For Reading Only

together	Queens
Bronx	Bulls
football	quarterback
goes	yards
chance	game
their	chances
snapping	planning
Sunday	looking
onto	ripped
boy	touchdown
boys	tackled

Word List 8 (sh), (ch),(-tch = /ch/), (qu = /kw/)

The Football Game

On Sunday, all the boys went to the park to play football. The Bronx Bulls were going to play the Queens Cubs. Hector, Tim, Nat, Jack, and Bill were on the Bulls. Hector was quarterback. He was not so good at stickball, but he was very good at football. Tim was quick, and he could catch a football. He had good hands. Whenever Hector would pass the ball to Tim, the ball would stick to Tim's hands. Nat was very quick, but he was not so good at catching a football. Jack was good at running with the ball. Big Bill was good at bumping. If Hector had the ball, and the boys from the Cubs wanted to get Hector, Bill could bump them so that Hector could run or pass.

The sun was out, but there was a wind. Ann, Jill and the girls were in the grandstand watching the game.

"Look at all the chicks in the grandstand," said Nat. "The girls look good in their slacks and caps."

Hector said, "You cannot look at the chicks, if we are going to win."

"Nat was not looking at *all* the girls," said Tim. "He was only looking at Ann. You know how much Nat likes Ann."

"Don't start with me," said Hector.

"Stop it," said Nat. "We have to stick together to win the game."

"OK," said Hector. Then Hector looked at Jack.

Jack said, "Sorry for snapping at you when we were playing stickball, Hector, but you did not have to run at me with the stickball bat."

Hector looked at Jack and said, "Sorry for saying I would crack the stickball bat on your lip, Jack, but you made me very mad. You are good at running with the ball. You know how to cut when you are running, and you are quick. I am with Nat: if we all stick together, we can win."

"Stop all this chatting!" called a boy from the Cubs. "We have to start the game."

The Bronx Bulls had to kick the ball to the Queens Cubs. Ann and Jill called out from the stands, "Go Bulls , Go! Go! Go Bulls go, Go!"

Bill kicked the ball. A boy from the cubs missed the ball and then picked it up. Tim ran and jumped on the boy, and he was down. The Cubs would have 4 chances to get a touchdown. A chance with the ball is called a down. The Cubs would have 4 chances, or 4 downs, to get a touchdown.

On 1st down, the Cubs did a running play. Mitch was a boy on the Queens Cubs. Mitch ran with the ball. Jack and Bill crashed into Mitch and tackled him. Mitch was down.

"Good going!" called Hector. "The Cubs did not even run an inch. I think they are going to pass now. We should rush the quarterback."

On 2nd down, the Cub quarterback drifted back to pass. Jack, Bill, and Hector rushed the quarterback. Bill ran to the Cub quarterback and jumped up to hit his hand, but the quarterback ducked and Bill missed. The quarterback passed the ball to Mitch. Mitch was running. Nat ran after Mitch. Nat was quick. Nat ran fast and jumped on Mitch, but Mitch would not go down. Tim was playing back. He ran and smashed into Mitch and Nat. They tackled Mitch, but the ball was six yards from a touchdown. Nat had a bad cut on his foot. He was limping.

"That cut is a bad gash," said Bill. "You will have to stitch it."

It was 3rd down. The Bulls had six yards to go for a touchdown.

"I have a hunch that the Cubs are going to run with the ball," said Hector. "If we bunch up on Mitch, I think we can stop the run."

On 3rd down, the Cub quarterback drifted back to pass and then handed the football to Mitch. Mitch ran and crashed into a bunch of Bulls. Mitch ran for only an inch and was down. The Cubs still had six yards to go for a touchdown.

"That was a good hunch you had, Hector," said Nat, who was still limping from the gash on his foot. "It is 4th down. If we stop them now, we will get the ball."

"They have to pass, now" said Hector. "I have a plan to trick them. We should bunch up so that we look like we are planning to stop a run, and then shift and go back to stop a pass."

There was a hush in the stands. It was 4th down and the Cubs still had six yards to go for a touchdown. The wind picked up, and there was a chill. Ann and Jill took out a quilt so they would not get chilled.

The Bronx Bulls bunched up like they wanted to stop a running play.

The Cub quarterback said, "The Bulls look like they plan to stop the run. We must pass the ball."

The Bulls were all bunched up to stop a running play, but then they shifted and went back to stop a pass. The Cub quarterback had wanted to do a running play, but when he saw the Bulls bunched up, he switched to a passing play. When the Cub quarterback saw the Bulls shift to stop a pass, he wanted to switch back to a run. The quarterback was all mixed up. He ran back and flipped a pass to Mitch. Mitch had the ball in his hands, but Nat punched the ball, and the football slipped out of his hands. Mitch did not catch the ball. The football was on the grass, and Hector jumped on the ball.

The Queens Cubs did not get a touchdown in 4 downs. They had 4 chances. Now the Bronx Bulls would get 4 chances for a touchdown.

Ann and Jill called out from the stands, "Go Bulls go, go! Go! Go Bulls go, Go!"

On 1st down, Hector went back to pass. Tim and Nat ran out to catch the pass. Hector passed the ball to Nat. The ball hit Nat in the chin, and the ball was on the grass. Nat did not catch it.

"You stink!" said Jack.

"Don't insult Nat," Hector said to Jack. "You think Nat stinks at catching a football, but your lips stink like a stinking fish! You should munch on some gum to stop your lips from stinking so much!"

"Shut up, you little shrimp, or I will punch you in the chin and kick you in the shin!" said Jack.

"I would punch you in the chin, but your chin has a rash on it. You look like a witch with an itch," said Hector.

"I quit!" said Jack.

"Jack, Don't quit!" said Nat. "And Hector, you shut up! Stop all this trash talk! We have to stick together! We cannot win if we start snapping."

"OK," said Hector. "I want to win this game. I want the Bulls to be champs! Jack, go out for a pass."

On 2nd down, Hector went back to pass. When the Cubs saw that Hector was going to pass, again, they rushed him. The Cubs put a big rush on Hector. Hector ducked as a Cub brushed by him. Then Hector slipped in the mud. The Cubs jumped on Hector. Mitch hit Hector's hand. He wanted to snatch the ball from Hector. Hector clutched onto the football so that the Cubs could not snatch the ball from him, but Hector was down. The Cubs had sacked the quarterback!

Some of the Cubs called out, "We sacked the quarterback!"

Hector was stuck in the mud. "This mud is like quicksand," said Hector. Hector punched his fist into his hand. He was mad. He did not like to get sacked.

Hector walked back to his friends. "Go out for a pass," he said.

Nat said, "No, Hector. We must not pass, again. We have to mix up the passing game with a running game. Hector, go back like you are going to pass, and then hand the ball to Tim for a run."

Hector went back to pass. Jack and Nat ran out, looking back as if they were going to catch a pass. The Cubs put on a big rush. They wanted to sack the quarterback, again. Hector handed the ball to Tim. The Cubs ran after Hector, but Hector did not have the ball. Hector tricked the Cubs. Tim was running with the ball. He was very quick. Mitch was the only Cub who could catch Tim. Big Bill bumped into Mitch. Mitch tripped in a ditch of mud. The Cubs could not catch Tim. He was too quick. Tim ran with the ball for a touchdown!

"Touchdown!" called Ann and Jill from the grandstand.

"Touchdown! Touchdown!" said Hector. "We are the champs!"

The Bronx Bulls were very glad to win the football game. After the game, Ann and Jill ran out of the grandstand to the boys. Nat would have to get a stitch to fix the cut on his foot. Hector had a bump on his lip. Hector's lip was stinging, and Nat was limping on his foot. Jack had a gash on his shin.

"We had fun," said Hector. "Jack, that gash on your shin looks like the rash on your chin. It is a very good match."

Jack looked mad. He was about to snap back at Hector.

"Don't get insulted, Jack" said Hector. "Don't be such a chump! I was only kidding."

"Did you call me a chump?" asked Jack.

"No, Jack," said Hector. "I did not wish to call you a chump. You look like a *chimp*! Would you like a banana?"

Ann gave Hector a pinch on his back.

"Stop playing!" said Ann. "You were glad to win the game. And now you are snapping. Quit snapping, or you and Jack will start swinging and punching."

"OK," said Hector "I will stop trashing Jack."

"Good," said Ann. "Walk with me to the truck for some lunch."

Ann and Hector walked to the lunch truck. Ann had a batch of shrimp, and Hector munched on fish and chips.

Hector and Ann walked to a tree and sat on a branch.

Ann said, "I have a chill from the wind." Hector put his hand on Ann's back.

Hector said, "The bump on my lip is still stinging from the football game."

"I can fix that," said Ann. Ann gave Hector a quick kiss on his lip.

"Thank you so much," said Hector with a blush. "That was such a good kiss that my lip is not stinging." Hector wanted to match Ann's kiss, but he slipped from the tree branch and hit the grass with a crash. Then he tripped in a ditch and ripped his pants. He had a bump on his lip and a cut on his chin. He would have to ask his mother to stitch his pants.

Hector was a champ at football, but he was not a champ at kissing Ann. No touchdown for Hector!

WORD LIST 9 (th [the], (th [thin], compound words)

that	thin	thankful	bathtub
this	with	thinks	withstand
then	within	things	bank
them	bath	bumps	suntan
	path	wash	catnap
	math	lived	dustpan
	thud	living	handstand
	sixth	thump	stickup
	fifth	thrill	handcuff
	thick	filth	handcuff
	thug		

For Reading Only

people	they
napping	ripped
dragged	butt
school	bathroom
	livingroom

Word List #9 (th, compound words)

In Handcuffs

Hector and Ann walked down the path that took them out of the park. Then they walked to the bus stop. The bus took them back to the street where they lived.

"I have to go back to my house," said Ann. "I don't want my mother to be mad at me." "Me, too," said Hector. "If my mother sees me like this, I am finished. She will kill me, if she sees the rip in my pants and the filth on my hands."

Hector ran back to his house. He wanted to take a bath and put on some good slacks so his mother would not see the filth on his hands and the rip in his pants. Hector went into his house. He was in luck. His mother was having a catnap in her room. Hector walked to his room. He was too quick, and he tripped on the rug with a thump and a thud.

"Is that you, Hector?" asked his mother.

"No," said Hector. "I'm still in the park. Go back to your catnap."

"*Hector!* Come in here, *now!*"

Hector walked into his mother's room. "Where were you?" asked his mother.

"I was in the park, playing football," said Hector.

"You are too thin to play football," Hector's mother said. "Look at you! Look at the filth on your hands and the mud on the floor! Your pants are ripped, and you have a bump on your lip and a cut on your chin."

"I do not think I am too thin to play football," said Hector. "It is a thrill for me to play football. I can withstand the hits and bumps of a football game. You should be thankful that I have a suntan from playing in the sun!"

"You should be thankful that I don't tan your thin little butt with my big thick hands! This is the fifth or sixth football game that you have come back with cuts, rips, and mud. Now get the dustpan! I do not want to see all this mud on the floor. Then get into the bathroom and wash that filth from your hands — and give me your pants! I have to stitch the rip."

Hector picked up the mud with the dustpan. Then he handed his mother his slacks and went into the bathroom. He took a bath in the bathtub. The suds made the cut on his chin sting. When he finished his bath, he went into his room to do some math for school.

When Hector finished his math for school, he went into the living room to talk to his mother. Hector was thinking about what Sam, the park man, had said about his father.

"Mother," said Hector, "why did Dad split? I know that Dad hit you. He hit me, too. But why did he walk out on us?"

"Why are you asking me now?" asked mother. "He is a no good thug! I do not like to talk about him! Have a nut bun and some milk!"

Hector had some nut buns with milk. Then Hector said, "Please talk to me, mother!"

"I do not wish to talk about your father! Have a nut bun."

"This is my fifth nut bun!" said Hector. "I do not want to have a sixth! I have to know about my father! I have to know!"

"Hector," his mother said, "your father did not walk out on you, or me. He did not just get up and split. He was dragged out of this house in handcuffs."

"Dad was dragged out of the house in handcuffs?" asked Hector. "**NO! NO!** Not my **Dad**! Not in handcuffs!"

"You wanted to know," said mother. "Now you know. He was a no good thug! I could withstand his hitting me, but I could not withstand his hitting you! You were just a little kid! When they dragged him out in handcuffs, I was glad."

"What did he do, mother?" asked Hector.

"He would mug people and stickup lunch stands. He would walk into a bank and say, "This is a stickup!" He was in the living room when they came and took him in handcuffs. You were in school. There was very little good within your father. I am glad he is out of the house and out of my life."

"But he is not out of *my* life," said Hector. "He is still my dad!"

WORD LIST 10 (Open Syllable at end of a word), (-y = long /i/).
 Reading rules: 1. When a vowel comes at the end of a word, the vowel makes a long sound (says its name) [we, no, jumbo].
2. 'Y' at the end of a one-syllable word has the sound of long /i / [my, by].

no	my	Hi
so	by	in fo
go	fly	al to
me	sky	buf fa lo
be	try	dis co
he	fry	jum bo
we	dry	lim bo
she	cry	brav o
ago	spy	stand by
also	sly	Fri day
see	pry	un til
tree	why	fris bee

For Reading Only

make	surprise	both	dance
feel	surprised	makes	without
feels	off		calypso

List #10 (Vowel at end of a word), (-y = long /i/)

Disco

Ann was in the park talking with her friend, Jill.
Jill asked, "Are you going to the disco on Friday?"
"No. I don't think so," said Ann.
"Why not?"
"Hector did not ask me out. I don't want to go to the disco without Hector."
"You can come with me," said Jill. "You do not have to go with a boy to go to the disco. We can do the limbo, and we can dance to some calypso."
"I am very good at limbo," said Ann, "but I cannot dance to calypso."
"You can try," said Jill.
"Are you going with a boy?" asked Ann.
"Yes," said Jill.
"Who are you going with?" asked Ann.
"Nat asked me six days ago, and I said yes."
"Do you like Nat?" asked Ann.
"Not so much," said Jill. "I wanted to go out with Jack, but he did not ask me. Nat is my standby. If Jack does not ask me, then I will go with Nat."
"If Jack asks you to go with him to the disco, are you going to ditch Nat and go with Jack, just like that?" asked Ann.
"I like Jack," said Jill. "Nat is only my standby. Why don't you ask Bill? He can be your standby, if Hector does not ask you."
"I am not going out with Buffalo Bill!" said Ann. "Buffalo Bill cannot do the limbo. If he puts his jumbo foot on my foot, I will be limping for six days. I do not want a standby. I do not want to ask Bill, and then ditch him for Hector. If Jack asks you to go to the disco, and you ditch Nat, Nat will cry. Girls like you make boys cry!"
"Girls like *me*?" asked Jill. "Don't even try it! You just called Bill a buffalo, just because he has a big fat jumbo foot!"
"I said that to *you*. I was only kidding. I would never say that to *Bill*."
"If you talk about Bill and call him jumbo or buffalo, he will know, "Jill said to Ann. "Then *you* will be the girl that makes a boy cry."
"OK," said Ann. "I should not talk about Bill like that, but why dump Nat for Jack? I don't want to pry, but what do you see in Jack?"
"When I am with Jack," said Jill, "I feel like I can fly in the sky."
"If you do go out with Jack, don't go with him to the hill in the park after the dance." kidded Ann.
"Why not?" asked Jill.
"You know what they say:

Jack and Jill went up the hill to try to hug and kiss,
All the girls went out to spy — this kiss they could not miss.
Jill did cry, when Jack did try, his lips were all so dry,
Jack did trip, and missed her lip, and kissed her in the eye.

"Bravo!" said Jill. "You can rap just like Nat, and for your info, you both stink at rap."

"For your info, Jill," said Ann, "I do not have to pry and ask you why you like Jack. You are just like Jack. Why don't you and Jack go up the tree on the hill, jump off, and see if you can fly in the sky?"

Just then Hector walked by with a frisbee in his hand. "What's up?" he asked.

"Jack and Jill are going *up* the tree on the hill."

"What?" asked Nat. "Are you and Jill snapping, again? You and Jill will never be good friends until you stop all this snapping."

"I have to go," said Jill, "but I think Ann is sad because she is not going to the disco on Friday." Jill walked down the path to the bus stop.

"You have to go to the disco!" Hector said to Ann.

"If you want me to go so much, why don't you ask me to go with you?" Ann started to cry. "You are going to go to the disco without me? Don't you want to dance with me? Don't you want to see me do the limbo?"

"Dry your eyes," said Hector. "I cannot dance with you at the disco because I am in the band. I will be playing the alto sax in the band. I am so good at playing calypso that they put me in the band six days ago. I wanted to surprise you! When I am up there playing my alto sax, I want to be looking at you."

Ann was surprised, and she was glad.

"Go run out and catch my frisbee!" said Hector.

Ann ran out, and Hector made the frisbee fly up in the sky. The frisbee landed in a tree. Hector was mad.

"Don't cry about a frisbee," Ann said to Hector.

"The only thing that would make me cry is if you don't come to see me play my sax at the disco."

"I will be there," said Ann. "Now, go up the tree and get the frisbee. Do not slip from the branch and rip your pants, or your mother will make you play your sax in your room for six days again!"

WORD LIST #11 (Silent e: a-e)

at	mad	lake	ape
ate	made	bake	tape
hat	fade	cake	shape
hate	blade	take	scrape
rat	grade	sake	case
rate	gave	wake	Jane
mat	cave	fake	shade
mate	wave	flake	trade
Kate	save	snake	blame
cap	shave	shake	shame
cape	grave	makes	became
Sam	brave	came	state
same	slave	game	pan cake
can	late	name	Batman
cane	gate	fame	be gan
past	date	frame	up date
paste	daze	flame	in sane
taste	gaze	names	nick name
male	blaze	face	make-up
female			

For Reading Only

goodbye
one
two
starting
grabbed
over
well
under

Word List 11 (Long *a*/ Silent *e*)

Shake to the Disco!

After school on Friday, all the kids went to the disco. Jill went to the disco with Nat. Tim came to the dance with Jane. Bill came without a date. Ann came to watch Hector play in the band. Hector picked up his alto sax and began playing with the band. The boys and girls started to dance. Just then, Jack walked in late with his date.

"Who is that girl with Jack?" asked Jill.

"I don't know her name," said Nat, "but she has a good-looking shape! Look at her shake!"

"Shut up, Nat," said Jill. Jill was mad because Jack came with a good-looking date. Jill grabbed Nat's hand and walked over to Jack and his date.

"Hello, Jack," said Jill.

"Hello, Jill," said Jack. "Hello Nat. This is my girl, Flame."

"Your *girl*? " asked Jill. "Is your girl's name *Flame*?"

"You don't like my name, Jane?" asked Flame.

"That's Jill! My name is ***Jill**!* "

"Well, if you don't like my name, *Jill*, you can jump in the lake!"

"***You*** can jump in the lake, snake!" said Jill. "I was only asking you if Flame is the name your mother gave you, or just your nickname."

"Flame is my name, Jane, and I have fame because of the shape of my good-looking frame – and don't talk about my *mother*!"

"Are you insane?" said Jill. "I was not talking about your mother." Then Jill said to Jack, "Jack, how can you go out with such a flake!"

"Flame has such a good-looking shape," said Jack. "You should see her dance and shake."

"She has a big shape because she ate too much shake and bake!" said Jill. "Her make-up looks like paste! She must scrape it on her face."

"Don't talk about my shape," Flame said to Jill. "You don't rate, and you don't pass the grade, because you have the shape of a pancake!"

"And you look like an ape!" said Jill. "Go shave your face!"

"Where is your cape?" said Flame. "You look like Batman!"

"You look like Batman's mother!" said Jill.

Flame was very mad. The shade of her face became like a blaze of flame.

"Chill, chill!" said Nat. "Just chill out! I wish I had the two of you on tape! You two act like you just came out of a cave! It would be a shame if some kid took out a blade because of all this snapping. I would hate to have to go visit you in your grave! Please, for my sake, stop all this name calling!"

Just then, Hector and the band began playing the limbo. Two girls took out a big cane for a limbo stick. The two girls looked the same. Both girls had a Batman cape on. They were twins. Nat took Jill by the hand and walked over to the limbo stick. He was looking at the twins. The twins were so good-looking that Nat was in a daze.

Jill said, "Don't gaze at the twins. Take my hand and go under the limbo stick with me. The limbo game is fun."

Nat and Jill went under the limbo stick, but Jill saw that Nat's gaze was on one of the twins as he went under the stick. After they went under the cane, Nat was still looking at one of the twins in a daze.

"Wake up, Nat!" said Jill. "You are in a daze! You look like you want to trade me for a twin with a fake Batman cape. You must be insane! You came with *me* to the disco!"

"Don't blame *me*," said Nat. "I will give you an update on what's up. You wanted to go to the dance with Jack. I was just your standby, in case Jack did not ask you out. You act like I am your slave. You are mad because you think Jack wants to make out with Flame. That's a shame!"

Nat gave Jill a wave and said, "Goodbye!" Then Nat walked out the door and past the gate. Nat sat down under a tree in the shade.

The band began to play calypso. Jill had no one to dance with, and she wanted to cry. Then Jill went over to Bill and asked him to dance.

One of the twins walked out the door, past the gate, and over to Nat, who was still sitting in the shade. The sun was going down, and the day was starting to fade. "Hi," she said. "My name is Kate. I saw you looking at me when you went under the limbo stick."

"Looking at you makes me feel good," said Nat. "I don't think there is one female in school as good-looking as you. Did you come with a date?"

"No, I don't have a date," said Kate. "Would you like to come back in and dance with me?"

"Did you just state that you don't have a date and you would like to dance with *me*?" asked Nat. "It would save my day, if I could dance with you!"

After the dance, Nat took Kate home. When they came to the door, Kate said, "Would you like to come in for some cake? You should taste the cake my mother baked."

"I would love to taste some cake," said Nat. Nat went in and ate some cake. When he finished the cake, he gave Kate a kiss goodbye and danced all the way home!

WORD LIST 12 (Silent e: i-e)

pin	Tim	size	five
pine	time	prize	dive
fine	dime	wise	drive
wine	dimes	wide	dived
mine	hide	side	bee hive
line	ride	slide	alive
vine	ripe	pride	life time
nine	life	bride	dis like
shine	wife	pile	in side
like	nice	file	out side
bike	die	mile	sun rise
hike	lie	smile	sun shine
Mike	bee	smiled	camp site
pike	grape	while	in vite
strike	grapes	pipe	in vited
bikes	shack	wipe	wind pipe
liked	sticks	swipe	hitch hike
bite	bass	stripe	crushed
bites	swim	striped	ar rive
puffed	stuff	pitched	ar rived grin

For Reading Only

blue
can't
our
God
next
housewife

Word List 12 (Long *i*, silent *e*).

A Dive in the Lake

The next day, Nat had a big wide smile on his face. "That was some dance!" he said to Hector.

"Oh, you liked the way I played the sax in the band?" asked Hector.

"I was not talking about you and the band," said Nat. "I was talking about the dance I had with Kate! She is good-looking on the outside, and a nice girl on the inside. Thinking of her makes me smile."

"I am glad you are not after Ann, because Ann is *my* girl."

"Ann is a fine girl," said Nat, "but she is not mine. I like Kate, now. I think I could be with Kate for life. Kate could be my bride. She could be my wife, and I could be her husband. She would make a good wife. Kate is so fine that I would be glad to be with her for a lifetime."

"Nat," said Hector, "are you insane? You talk like you had too much wine. What you are saying is way out of line. You are still in school and living with your mother, and so is Kate! You and Kate are still kids! Kate does not want to be a housewife, and you don't have a dime to your name. The time is not ripe to start thinking about a bride. I do not think it would be wise to take a wife at your age. Take what you said and file it!"

"I know," said Nat with pride. "I just think that Kate is a prize. She is the sunshine of my life."

"Stop all this jive talk. Today is Sunday. The dance was on Friday. You only know Kate for two days. I think you are insane."

Just then, Tim came by on his bike.

"Are you going on the school trip? asked Tim.

"What trip?" asked Nat and Hector.

"The two day camping trip to Surprise Lake," said Tim. "All the kids in our class are invited. We will be going in nine days. We can fish and hike, and play in the sun. We can ride on bikes and sing at the campsite. We don't have to hitchhike to get there. Sam said we will get there in a school bus."

"I like to hike, fish, and play in the sun," said Nat, "but I dislike going on a school bus."

"If you dislike the school bus so much, you can hitchhike to the campsite," kidded Hector.

Nine days passed, and it was time for the class to go on the camping trip. Hector, Ann, Nat, Jill, Tim, Bill, Jack, Mike, and Kate were all going on the camping trip. Sam, the park man, went with the class. Flame did not go with them because she was not from their school.

The class went on the bus at sunrise. It was a 60 mile drive to Surprise Lake, and they did not arrive at the campsite until nine. It was a nice day. There was sunshine on the pine trees. The sky was blue. The wide lake was sky-blue.

Next to the lake was a vine. There were grapes on the vine. The grapes looked like they could make a very nice wine.

"Don't swipe the grapes," said Sam. "You could get a fine. When the grapes on the vine are ripe, they will be picked and crushed for wine."

"Look at the size of that beehive on that branch on the pine tree!" called Mike. "Watch out! You don't want a bee to sting you!"

Sam took out his pipe and called out, "Boys, take the cabin by the pine trees. Girls, take the cabin by the grape vine. Go get your things off the bus, and bring them inside your cabin."
Hector and Nat walked over to the cabin by the grape vine. "Can we hide in here?" Hector asked the girls.

"Sorry, Hector," said Ann. "We cannot invite you in, now."

"We will see you in a little while, Nat," said Kate with a smile.

"Come on kids!" called Sam. "Put your stuff in the cabin, grab a fishing stick at the shack, and go down to the lake. We are going fishing!"

"I hate fishing," said Jill.

"We have to catch some pike fish or striped bass for lunch," said Sam. "Try it. Fishing can be a pile of fun."

All the kids ran into the shack to pick up fishing sticks, and then ran down to the lake and began to fish. Jack pitched a dime into the lake. "Look at the fish go after the dime," he said.

"Don't pitch dimes into the lake!" said Sam. "If a fish bites the dime, it will die!"

Jack had five dimes. He began to pitch them into the lake one at a time.

Hector ran over to Jack and said, "Sam said you will kill the fish if you pitch dimes in the lake!"

"I want to see the fish bite … and die," Jack said with a smile.

"Wipe that grin off of your face!"

Hector gave Jack a push. Jack lifted his hand to strike Hector with his fist. Hector ducked and punched Jack on his side. Jack grabbed Hector, and Hector tripped over a fishing line. The two of them slid into the lake.

Jill called out, "Jack can't swim! He is under the water!"

Mike dived into the Lake, and Hector and Mike dragged Jack out of the lake.

"Lie him on his back," said Jill. "Please don't die!" Jill put her lips on Jack's lips and puffed into Jack's windpipe. Jack spit out some water and looked up at Jill.

"Thank God you are alive!" she said.

WORD LIST 13 (u-e)

us	June	pure
use	tune	cure
fuse	fume	sure
cut	nude	im pure
cute	dude	in jure
tub	rude	fig ure
tube	crude	assure
cub	mule	ex cuse
cube	rule	ab use
dude	rules	saved
mutt	cubes	died
mute	ice	stu pid
flute	brute	in clude
killed	prune	at ti tude
puff	prunes	

For Reading Only

pushed
gets
hot
full
short
many

WORD LIST 13 (u-e)

Excuse Me!

"Where am I?" Jack asked as he looked up at Jill. "I feel like a mutt that just came out of a tub of ice cubes. I wish it was a hot day in June."

"Mike and Hector just dragged you out of the lake," said Jill. "You and Hector were pushing and punching, and you both slipped into the lake. You cannot swim without a tube, so you went under the water. I was sure you were going to die. I told them to lie you on your back I put my lips on your lips and puffed into your windpipe. When you looked up at me, I was so glad that I wanted to sing a tune or play the flute."

Jack was mute. He could not say a thing.

Ann said, "Don't be mute like a stupid mule. Talk to us!"

"I do not like your attitude," said Jill. "It was rude of you to call Jack a stupid mule. Your Hector is a stupid brute. Hector started pushing, and they slipped into the lake. Jack could have died."

"Sorry," said Ann. "It was rude of me to call Jack a mule, but don't call Hector a stupid brute. Hector just dragged Jack out of the lake. He saved Jack's life. Make sure to include that when you talk about Hector."

Jack was mad and he began to fume: "How could you say that Hector saved my life! He gets mad too fast! He has a short fuse, and he could have killed me over some stupid fish! I will get him for this!" Then Jack looked at Jill and said, "It was not Hector that saved my life. My cure came from the puff of your pure cute lips."

"Excuse me!" said Jill. "If you think my lips are so cute and pure, then why did you take Flame to the dance last Friday? My lips are pure, but Flame's lips are so impure that she would kiss a mule, if it was male."

"I assure you, Jill," said Jack. "I wanted to take you to the dance, but Flame asked me to take her. She has such a nice figure, I had to say yes. I just could not stop thinking about how she must look in the nude."

Jill slapped Jack in the face and she said, "Jack, you are as crude as a dude on a big fat stinking mule!" Then Jill pushed Jack back into the lake.

Jack could stand up in the water this time, but he had mud all over his face. "You do not have to abuse me because I went to the dance with Flame," he said. "Look at the cut on my foot! Did you have to injure me? I only wanted to use Flame. I assure you that you are the only girl I love."

Jill looked at Jack and said, "You're full of it. I think you ate too many prunes."

"Don't be mad at me, Jill," said Jack. "I will never see Flame again! But is there a rule that says I can't even *think* about her?"

WORD LIST 14 (short 'o')

ox	job	hat	song
box	sob	hit	long
fox	mob	hut	off
on	slob	hot	odd
not	snob	tap	rock
cot	hop	top	lock
lot	cop	tip	clock
dot	pop	fax	sock
tot	stop	fix	shock
got	mop	fox	block
rot	shop	nut	socks
spot	drop	not	loc king
hog	flop	rib	tick-tock
log	slop	rob	frog man
jog	blond	cap	sand box
frog	pond	cup	pad lock
Tom	rod	cop	cry ing
mom	nod	cops	sur vive
boxing	God	upon	bot tom

For Reading Only

he'll   getting   listen   something   cool

you'll   dripping   listening   nothing   ones

other   steps   woods   swimming   most

been

Word List 14 (short 'o')

Locked Up by a Cop

Jack was dripping water from top to bottom.

"You look like a dripping mop," said Jane. "Go dry off. You don't want to get sick."

Jack took his fishing rod and went back to his cabin to dry off. He took off his socks, slacks, and cap, and put on dry ones. Jack did not want to look like a slob. He put his dripping slacks and socks on the side of his cot to dry.

Mike came into the cabin and walked over to Jack. "Hector was not the only one to drag you out of the lake. I did too! You did not even thank me!"

"Oh, sure. Thanks a lot, Mike," said Jack.

"Come outside," said Mike. "Sam wants to rap with all of us."

When Mike and Jack got outside, all the kids were sitting on a log. Sam sat on a box and began to talk. "Things are out of hand," he said. "When I saw Hector and Mike drag Jack out of the lake, I was in shock. If not for Jill's quick thinking, Jack would have died. We should all thank God that Jack is still alive. A lot of you kids live on the same block. You have got to know how not to get other kids mad, what to say when they *do* get mad, and what to do when *you* get mad. If you don't figure out how to do this, you will not survive!"

Tim said, "What do you want us to do — just stand there and take it if a kid starts up? Last June I was jumped by this big kid, Tom. What do you want me to do while he is punching me — should I say, 'Hi Tom, can we talk?' No way!"

"I am not saying that you should talk to a kid while he is punching you. There are times when you have to hit back — or run. But most of the time, people only start hitting when they are mad. A lot of the time, you can cool the other dude down. If a kid says something that makes you mad, tell him how you feel."

"If a dude snaps on my mom, my fist will tell him how I feel," said Hector.

"And if the dude stabs you, and your mom has to see you go into your grave, how do you think your mom will feel then?" asked Nat. "To use your fist every time a dude says something stupid … is stupid!"

Sam said, "This is what you can do to tell a kid why you are mad at him without getting into a boxing match. There are 4 steps:

1. Ask him if you can talk to him.
2. Say something nice, like "We have been friends for a long time."
3. Tell him how you feel and why.
4. Thank him for listening.

"Only a nut would try this," said Hector.

"Good," said Sam. "You are just the nut I want to act this out. You have to insult Nat, and then Nat has to tell you how he feels without getting you mad."

"Oh, this is going to be fun," said Hector. "Hi Nat. You stink like a frog that ate fish rot from a pond, and your father looks like Frogman!"

"I'm going to sock you in the lip!" said Nat.

Sam had to grab Nat to stop him from punching Hector. "This is only an act, Nat," said Sam.

"But you did not say that Hector could snap on my *father!*"

"Tell that to Hector, but use the steps. If you tell Hector that you are going to sock him in the lip, you will get him mad, and things will get hot. You want to tell him how you feel without starting a boxing match."

"OK," said Nat. [Step #1] "Hector, can I talk to you?"

"Sure," said Hector. "What's up?"

[Step #2] "You and I have been friends for a long time," said Nat. "We have played football and stickball together. We had fun when we went to shop for my fishing rod. But I do not like it when you snap on me."

"Get a life, Nat!" said Hector. "I was only playing. You don't stink like a frog. You only look like a frog, but you stink like a hog."

[Step #3] "Stop playing," said Nat. "It makes me mad. You should not have snapped on my father. Snapping on my pop makes me fume."

"Sure, Nat," said Hector. "I am sorry about snapping on your father."

[Step #4] "Thanks for listening," said Nat. "Please don't do it again."

"That was good!" said Sam. "Now switch. Nat will insult Hector, and Hector will tell Nat how he feels without getting Nat mad."

"Can I insult Hector with a long rap song?" asked Nat.

"Sure!" said Sam with a nod. "Just make sure this rap is not a flop!"

Nat did this rap song about Hector:

"Come on down and listen to my song,
It's a rap about Hector, and it's not too long.
Hector thinks like a fox, and he looks like an ox,
But he acts like a little tot playing in a sandbox.

One day Hector was swimming in the pond.
He said, "Look at that girl, I think she's a blond.
But isn't it odd, she's sitting on a log."
Too bad Hector, your girl is a frog.

Hector saw the female frog hop on top of a log.
He swam to the sand, and started to jog.
The sun was hot, and he wanted to stop,
But his foot hit a rock, and he began to hop.

The frog said, "Look at that frogman hop upon the sand."
She jumped on Hector and kissed him on his hand.
The frog got sick and spit up some slop,
She said, "Hector makes me sick, he stinks like a mop."

Now Hector is the man, he will hit you on the spot,
You can be as big as an ox, or just a little tot.
But if Hector sticks to hitting, he'll be in for a shock.
A cop will lock him in a room with a big padlock,
And he'll have nothing to do but listen to the clock,
Tick-tock, tick-tock, Hector and the clock.

So listen to me Hector: don't be a snob,
Stop hitting on your friends, go to school, get a job.
Don't rob with the mob, and you'll never have to sob.
The only thing to cry about is — you look like a frog!

Hector was very mad.

[Step #1] "I have to talk to you, Nat." he said.

[Step #2] "You and I have been good friends for a long time, [Step #3] but I am very mad at you, now. I know you were only playing Sam's game. It's OK that you kidded me about all that frog stuff, but you did not have to talk about cops locking me up in a room with a padlock. My father is doing time! The cops locked him up. All he does is look at the clock. I hate you for saying that!" Hector began to sob. He could not stop crying.

"Sorry, Hector," said Nat. "I did not know about your pop. Please forgive me."

"Sure," said Hector with a sniff. [Step #4] "Thanks for listening."

Then Hector grabbed Ann's hand and ran into the woods.

WORD LIST 15 (o-e)

hop	con	hole	con vict
hope	cone	pole	fall ing
cop	bone	stole	a rose
cope	lone	dove	a lone
mope	zone	drove	rocks
rope	stone	cove	tie
not	rod	stove	on to
note	rode	nose	safe
vote	code	rose	place
rob	woke	hose	try ing
robe	poke	those	stick ing
globe	coke	chose	a while
rope	choke	close	sig nals
dope	smoke	doze	pro pose
slope	broke	froze	sup pose
home	spoke	small	im pose
van	joke	joked	va nil la

For Reading Only

far	help	climb	Let's
cook	find	climbing	coming
dark	S-O-S	climbed	stopped
dog	vanilla	mountain	

Word List 15 (o-e)

Without a Rope

"Where are we going?" asked Ann, as Hector took Ann by the hand and ran into the woods.

"Out of here!" said Hector. "I am so mad at Nat I could choke him! I know what he said was only a joke, but he was a dope to rap about a cop locking me up! All that made me think of my pop. Nat is my friend, but sometimes he makes me so mad I want to poke him in the nose. I have to go to a place where I can cool off."

"I am glad you chose not to poke Nat in the nose," said Ann, "but why do we have to run off into the woods? We should go back."

"No!" said Hector. "If I go back, all the kids will start asking me about my father. They will ask me, 'Did he rob a lunch truck?' Some kids say he stole $50 bills from a bank — 'Did he give you some? Did the cops take him in handcuffs?' I could not cope with all that. I could not stand it if my friends called my pop a convict or a con. If you want to go back, Ann, you can go."

"No, Hector," said Ann. "I do not want you to be in the woods all alone. I will go with you, but I hope you don't go too far into the woods."

"Let's take the path up this slope," said Hector. "I think we can see the lake from the top of the mountain. It's not too far."

Hector and Ann began to hike up and up the slope. Ann slipped on a stone, but Hector grabbed her by the hand to stop her from falling. When they got to the top, there was a side path that led to some big rocks. Hector and Ann walked down the path and sat on the rocks. From there, they could see the blue-green water of the lake.

"From up here, it looks like we are on top of the globe," said Hector. Hector began to hop from rock to rock.

"Look!" said Ann. "I can see the kids sitting on a log by the cabin. Do you see the smoke? I think the smoke must be coming from the stove in the cabin. Sam must be cooking the pike fish and striped bass we got from the lake with our fishing rods."

"I hate fish," said Hector.

"It's not so bad. If you catch the fish and cook it on the same day, the fish does not stink."

"I think I could bite into some fish, now," said Hector. "All I had today was a banana. I could even bite into a dog bone!"

"I wish I had a lunch box," said Ann. "I would love to have some ham and a coke."

"I wish I had a vanilla cone and a glass of coke," said Hector.

"Don't be a stupid dope, Hector," said Ann. "Let's go down the path and have some lunch."

"OK," said Hector, "but I propose that we climb down the rocks. It will be fast if we climb down. If we take the path, we will be too late for lunch."

"I don't know," said Ann. "It's not safe. We can slip on those rocks."

"Come on, Ann," said Hector as he arose from where he was sitting.

"Let's climb down."

"Can we take a vote?" asked Ann.

"I suppose so," said Hector. "But if it's a tie, we climb down. I vote 'Yes'. You oppose climbing down, so you vote 'No'. It's a tie! We climb down the rocks! When we get to the bottom, I will give you a rose."

Ann looked at Hector and said, "Take note of this! I propose that you wash your face with a cold water hose! Wake up! I chose to hike back down the path in the woods. You cannot impose your will on me with this joke of a vote!"

"OK," said Hector. "Then I will climb down alone!" Hector began to climb down the rocks.

"Don't make me go down the path in the woods all alone!" called Ann. "I cannot cope with walking in the woods all alone. I will go with you down those rocks. I just hope it's safe."
Ann started to climb down. She put her foot on a small rock, but the rock gave way. Ann began to slide. "Help! Help!" she called.

Ann slid down the rocks and bumped into Hector. They both were now slipping down the mountain. A lone tree was sticking out by a rock nine yards down. The tree had a branch that stuck out like a pole over the rocks. Hector grabbed onto the branch with one hand and onto Ann with the other. They stopped their slide just in time. There was a cliff with a 200-yard drop after that tree. Ann and Hector froze. They could not climb down or up.

Just then, Hector saw a hole next to one of the rocks. The hole was the size of a pinhole. Hector broke a small branch off the tree and began to poke at the hole. Then Ann and Hector began to dig with their hands. They dug and dug. After awhile, the hole on the side of the mountain became very big.

"Look, Hector!" said Ann. "It's a cave! We can go into the cave and be safe for a while."

Hector and Ann climbed into the cave. They were in the cave for a long time. The sun was going down, and it was getting dark. Hector began to mope. "If we had a rope, we could climb down," he said. "I wish we had a rope."

"You were a dope to climb on rocks without a rope," said Ann. "We will never get down from here! It's getting dark, and it's getting cold. I just wish we could make some smoke. We could make smoke signals in S-O-S code. But even if we could, it's too dark now to see smoke signals. Sam and the kids must be looking for us by now, but they will never find us in the dark. I want to go home! I want to go home!" Ann began to cry.

Hector sat down next to Ann and gave her a hug. "We will get down," he said. "Trust me." Then Hector took Ann's hand and said, "Thank you for coming with me. It's good to know that I have a friend I can trust to stick by me." Then Hector lifted Ann's chin with his hand to give her a kiss. Hector's face came close to Ann's, but it was too dark in the cave for Hector to see Ann's face. So he missed her lips and kissed her on the nose.

"I did not know that you were in love with my nose," joked Ann.

"I was trying to find your lips, but it is too dark in this cave," said Hector.

Ann spoke to Hector and said, "I don't think this is the time or the place for kissing. It's getting dark, and there is a chill in the cave. I wish I had my robe to put on my back."
"You don't have your robe," said Hector, "but I can rub your back."

Hector rubbed Ann's back to help her with the cold. After awhile, Hector and Ann began to doze off. Hector began to think about how he and Mike dove into the lake to save Jack. Hector did not know why he dove into the lake to save Jack. He just did. Then Hector began to think about a time when he rode in a van with his father and mother. His father drove the van to a cove to go swimming. Hector's father dove into the water, but he could not swim. Hector was too small to dive into the water to save his father. Hector began to call out, "My father can't swim! My father can't swim!"

Ann woke up and gave Hector a shake. "Wake up! Wake up!" she said to Hector.

Hector woke up and said, "Where am I? Where am I?"

It was pitch black in the cave when Hector and Ann woke up.

WORD LIST 16 (igh = long i)

sky	light	mid night
high	slight	to night
thigh	flight	flash light
sigh	right	light ning
sight	bright	up right
night	fright	night mare
might	lights	grope
tight	sun light	mis take
fight	in sight	in sist
fight ing	de light	in sist ing

For Reading Only

great	daylight	lost
though	outright	front
saving	sleep	loved
didn't	another	first
almost	someone	used
		nowhere

Word List 16 (igh = long i)

Midnight in a Cave

"Ann? Is that you?" asked Hector.

"Yes," said Ann. "We must have dozed off. I think you were having a nightmare. You were calling out in your sleep, 'My father can't swim! My father can't swim!'"

"I know my father can swim," said Hector, "but in my nightmare, he was going down in the water. I could not save him. I saved Jack in the water, and I hate Jack, but I could not save my father."

"You did the right thing when you saved Jack's life, even though you dislike him," You would like to save your father, but you cannot. Your father can swim in a lake, but he cannot swim in life. So the cops took him and locked him up. You want to help your father, because you love him, but you cannot save him. You feel bad because you could save someone you hate, but not someone you love. In your nightmare, you mixed up saving Jack in the water with saving your father. You are a very good kid, Hector, and I love you."

"You have good insight into my nightmare," Hector said to Ann. "You are the only one who can see how I feel inside. I love you, too, Ann, and right now I feel like kissing you, but it is so dark in here I might miss your lips and kiss you on the nose again."

"It is so dark in this stupid cave," said Ann, "you can't even tell if I'm sitting or standing."

"That's right," said Hector. "If I try to kiss you now, I might miss your lips and kiss you on the butt."

"This is not the time to joke," said Ann. "I don't like the dark. It must be midnight. Being in a cave at night is like being in a nightmare. When you woke me up by calling out in your sleep, I had a big fright. I could not see the hand in front of my face. I am talking to you, but I can't see you. It is as if I lost my sight."

"I wish we were back in the daylight up high on top of the rocks," Hector said with a sigh. "It was a great sight to look down on the sky-blue lake from so high up."

"It was a great sight looking down at the lake from high up," said Ann, "but did you have to climb down those rocks! It was not very bright of you to do that. I told you to take the path in the woods. I said it was not safe to climb down the rocks, but you would not listen to me. Now I cannot see the hand in front of my face! You made a big mistake!"

"You did not have to climb down with me," said Hector. "*You* are the one who slipped. If I didn't grab onto you and the tree branch, we both would have slipped off the cliff. You should thank me, and not blame me!"

"Thank you?" asked Ann. "I suppose I should thank you for passing the night with me in a cave without even a flashlight! I suppose I should thank you because I almost froze in my sleep tonight! I suppose I should thank you for insisting that I climb down those stupid rocks!"

"I didn't insist that you climb down the rocks, That is an outright lie!"

"No it's not! You made me go down! You made me!"

"I did not!"

"Yes you did!"

"I did not! Don't blame me!"

"Look at us!" said Ann. "A little while ago I said I loved you, and you said you loved me. And now look at us! We are fighting!"

"I wish I could look at us fighting," joked Hector. "I can't even see your face or my hand. How can I look at us fight?"

"Please, Hector," said Ann. "I do not want to fight with you. Slide next to me and take my hand."

Hector slid next to Ann and took her hand. Then he gave her a hug.

"Hug me tight," said Ann. "I do not like to fight at night, and I hate the dark. I cannot stand it in this cave. Let's get out of here."

"I still have the small branch we broke off from the tree to dig into this cave," said Hector. "We can use it to feel our way in the dark."

Hector began to feel his way with the branch, and Ann used her hands to feel her way on the side of the cave.

"I think the way out of the cave is this way," said Hector.

"No," said Ann. "I think the way out is to the right."

Hector and Ann began to grope in the dark. They made a right and then another right, but they could not find the way out. They wanted to go back to where they had started, but they could not find the way back. Hector and Ann were lost in the dark cave."

"I wish we had a flashlight," said Hector. "I cannot see without a light."

Ann slapped her thigh and said. "A light! A light! I have a match box! We can light a match!"

"A match?" asked Hector with a big smile. "You had a match all this time? Why didn't you say so? Light it up!"

Ann took out a match and lit it. The first thing Hector saw was Ann's eyes. Hector gazed into her eyes and said, "It is a delight to look into your eyes again."

"It would be a delight for me to look into your eyes, too, but not from the flame of a match. I want to see your face in the sunlight!" said Ann."

"First, we have to find a way out of here," said Hector,

Just then, the match went out. It was pitch black in the cave again.

"Do you have another match?" asked Hector.

"Yes," said Ann.

"We can light up the branch with your match," said Hector. "A flame from a branch will not go out so fast."

Ann lit another match, and Hector took the match and lit the tip of the branch. In a little while, the branch was in flame, and its light was as bright as lightning that lights up the sky on a dark night.

"Let's go fast! This flame will not last long," said Ann.

Hector and Ann were walking fast, now. They took a right and began to go down a slight slope. The cave was cold and damp, and the way out was nowhere in sight. At times, the top of the cave was not high, and they could not stand upright. After a long while, they came to a big hall. The top of the cave was very high in the hall, and they could now stand upright. Water was dripping from rocks that were high up on the walls of the cave. That made them think that they had to have something to drink, so they let some of the water drip on their lips.

Hector and Ann were far from where they had started. The flame that had lit their way was getting small, and they were lost. Ann began to cry. "We will never get out of here," she said. "The flame is about to go out, and we don't have another match. We are going to die in this cave! They will never find us! They don't even know we are in here! I don't want to die! I don't want to die!"

"Don't give up," said Hector, trying to act brave. "It will be all right." But Hector was thinking that he had made a big mistake to take flight into the woods in the first place. He was thinking that he should have faced up to what his friends might have said about his father. It did not help to run off.

Just then, the flame from Hector's branch went out.

"We are finished!" said Ann. "We will never see sunlight again!"

WORD LIST#17 (short e)

egg	get	men	tell	let's
beg	pet	pen	fell	fresh
big	met	den	yell	neck
log	let	hen	yelled	bobcat
leg	jet	ten	smell	e ven
bat	net	then	shell	rob in
bit	vet	them	end	o pen ing
but	yet	rest	bend	kit ten
bet	red	best	lend	up set
six	bed	pest	send	sun set
sex	led	west	spend	tun nel
pop	fed	vest	spent	my self
pup	wed	test	dent	him self
pep	sped	nest	bent	pen cil
step	fled	chest	went	back pack
yes	felt	desk	tent	fam ished
mess	left	help	vent	pres ent
less	melt	held	rent	sketch
legs	belt	dim	tenth	stretch
	eggs		be fore	sud den

For Reading Only

baby	yourself
any	pulled
more	hiking
stay	

Word List #17 (short e)

This is the End!

"This is the end!" said Ann. "We will never get out of this cave."

"I bet we will get out of here, yet," Hector said as he looked into Ann's eyes. "Don't be upset. You have to trust me."

Ann looked back into Hector's eyes, and started to yell, "Your eyes! Your eyes! I can see your eyes!"

"And I can see your nose!" yelled Hector. "And your neck, and your legs, and the vest on your chest."

"Don't be fresh!" said Ann.

"I'm not being fresh," said Hector. "I can see you! The flame is out, and I can still see you!"

"I know!" yelled Ann with a sudden rush of pep. "There must be an opening that is letting light into the cave!"

"Let's go find it!" said Hector.

The light was coming from a tunnel. Hector and Ann could not walk too fast in the dim light of the tunnel. The tunnel bent to the left, and then led to another hall.

"Look!" said Ann. "A kitten! And look over there — another one! There are six of them. Can I take one home as a pet? I can beg my mother for a pet cat. If I take it to the vet, my mom will let me have it as a pet. Mom said she would let me have a pup. I am sure she would let me have a little cat, if I beg her for one."

Ann picked up a kitten and said, "Look at this cute baby cat."

"What sex is it?" asked Hector.

"It's a baby female cat," said Ann.

"It's a female, but it is not a baby house cat," said Hector. "I think it is a bobcat! This end of the cave must be the den of a bobcat. Put the baby bobcat down, and let's get out of here fast! If its mother comes back and sees us in here with her kittens, she will be very mad!"

Just then, there was a big cry. It was the call of the mother bobcat.

"The mother bobcat is coming back to her den!" said Ann. "Look! She is over there! She is as big as ten house cats! Let's run for it!"

Ann and Hector fled down another tunnel. The light in the tunnel was getting bright. There was an opening in the cave that led to the outside. The bobcat sped after them, but when Ann and Hector climbed out of the cave, the bobcat stopped and went back to her kittens.

Hector and Ann had to bend a lot when they ran in the tunnel. They were glad to be standing upright, again, under a bright blue sky. Hector put his hands up high, and began to stretch. Then Ann started to stretch her legs and her neck. Then she said, "It feels like we have just passed a big test. We have made it out of the cave alive!"

"Look, Ann," said Hector. "We must have made our way to the other side of the mountain. We are still up high, but we cannot see the lake. We must be looking west. The lake has to be on the other side. I think it will be best if we go to the top of the mountain. We should see the lake from there and find a path back down to the camp.

"Well, I don't want to be a pest," said Ann, "but I cannot take another step. I want to rest awhile."

"We can't do that," said Hector. "The bobcat might come back."

"I don't think so," said Ann. "Bobcats only come out at night."

"All right," said Hector. "We can rest for a little while, but I want to get back to the campsite. I would love to be fed a little bit of food and something to drink. I would love to rest on a bed in a cabin, or even on a mat in a tent. I bet you would too."

"Yes," joked Ann. "I wish I could be fed some hot food in bed, but you can stay by yourself on a mat in a tent. As for myself, I'll take the bed in the cabin."

"Look at that tree," said Hector. "There is a nest in that branch. It's not too high. I can climb up and take a look at it." Hector climbed up the tree to look at the nest. Inside the nest were six blue eggs. Hector picked up an egg and held it in his hand.

"I think this is a robin egg," said Hector.

"You should not pick up an egg from a nest," said Ann. "The mother robin can tell the smell of your hand on her egg. The hen will be very upset."

"Now I have a mother robin and a mother bobcat mad at me," said Hector. "Let's go!"

Just then, the egg slipped from Hector's hand and fell onto Ann's leg. The egg broke and made a mess on her leg.

"I think I made a dent in the shell when the egg fell," said Hector.
"It's not a little dent," said Ann. "The shell is cracked, and my leg is a mess. I should take a bat and crack an egg on *your* leg!"

Ann felt bad about the mess on her leg, but she was more upset that the nest had one less egg. "The hen is going to miss her egg," she said.

"The hen still has five eggs," said Hector. "So what if she has one less! I wish I had some ham and eggs."

"And you were mad at Jack because he pitched dimes in the lake that could kill a fish?"

"You are right," said Hector. Hector felt a bit sad, but there was nothing he could do that would help the mother robin or the egg that smashed onto Ann's leg. Hector pulled in his belt to make it tight, and began thinking about ham and eggs, and a glass of coke.

"I am famished," said Hector. "We have not had any food in over a day. Men cannot live without food. The only thing we had to drink was some dripping water in the cave."

"This is about the tenth time you have talked about food," said Ann. "I am famished, too. We have to find a path back to the campsite before sunset. I don't want to get stuck in the woods at night."

Hector and Ann climbed to the top of the mountain. From the top, they could see the lake, again, and the path that led back to the campsite. Ann took out a pen, pencil, and a pad from her backpack, and began to sketch a tent and a log cabin that was next to the lake.

"I wish I had a desk to rest my pad on while I sketch," said Ann.

"I will lend you my desk when we get back, or send you a desk for a present," joked Hector, "but this is not the time to sketch with pencil or pen. I did not climb back up this mountain to get a suntan, and you did not come up here to sketch. I am famished. You did say you wanted to make sure we got back before sunset."

"You are right," said Ann. As she looked up, a jet that sped by in the sky. "We must be getting back, but I will miss being up here with you all alone. We spent the night in a cave, and it felt good to spend so much time together."

Hector began to blush, and his face became red. He was glad that he and Ann had met. He was thinking to himself about what it would be like to be wed to Ann.

Just then, Ann saw some men and kids hiking up the mountain. "Look," said Ann, "they must be looking for us."

"Hello!" called Ann and Hector. "We are over here!"

In a little while, Sam, two cops, and all the kids had climbed to the top of the mountain. "Where have you been?" asked Jack. "Did you find your pop?"

"No," Hector said to Jack, "but we did find your mother! She is living in a very nice box in the woods. We spent the night with her."

The cops held Jack back to stop him from punching Hector.

"We almost got killed up here," Ann yelled to Jack, "and the first thing out of your lips is a crack about Hector's father! You stink!"

Hector and Ann did not say another thing as they all hiked down the path back to the campsite.

WORD LIST 18 (e–e)

here	these	pet
mere	Chi nese	Pete
plate	Jap an ese	Pete's
plates	o bese	com pete
rice	e ven ing	com plete
gas	con test	con crete
soft	cot ton	ath lete
soft ball	a cross	ex treme
kept	boxed	ex pect ing
	kitch en	

For Reading Only

ears	near
keep	keeping
eating	beans
thanked	forever
three	along
added	pitcher

Word List #18 (e-e)

Pete's Rice and Beans

When Ann and Hector got back to the campsite, Ann asked Sam if he had any food. "We are famished," she said. "We did not have any food for over a day. Can we have something to eat and drink?"

"Go into that cabin over there," said Sam. "Pete, the camp cook, will give you some lunch."

Ann and Hector walked across the concrete where some boys were playing softball. Tim was at bat, and he hit the ball far.

"Tim is a good athlete," said Ann. "He is good at football and softball."

"I'm a good athlete, too," said Hector. "I am just as good at football and softball as Tim. I would love to compete with Tim in a softball hitting contest."

"Sure," said Ann, "but I think we should eat first."

Hector and Ann walked over to the cabin. Pete's pet dog was sitting outside. Hector and Ann went inside. The cabin had a kitchen and a big room for eating. Pete looked like he was expecting someone.

"What would you like?" asked Pete. "I have been expecting you."

"Do you have any Chinese food?" asked Ann.

"Or Japanese food?" added Hector.

"Where do you think you are?" asked Pete. "You eat what I give you! All I have is rice and beans. If you don't like it, get out!"

"I love rice and beans!" said Ann.

"Me, too!" said Hector.

"Then sit down over here," said Pete. "I will bring you a plate of rice and beans."

"Can we have some water?" asked Ann.

"Or a soft drink?" added Hector. "I would love to have a coke!"

"If you want a drink," said Pete, "fill up a pitcher of water at the sink."

Pete handed Hector and Ann two plates of rice and beans, and two cups for the pitcher of water. Hector and Ann ate their rice and beans and finished off the pitcher of water. Hector asked for another plate, and then another.

"If you keep eating like this, you will get obese," joked Ann.

"Today I can compete in an eating contest," joked Hector. "One more plate of rice and beans, Pete!"

"That's it for you!" said Pete. "It is not good to go from one extreme to the other extreme. If you are famished, you should not try to stuff yourself. You could get sick. This is not an eating contest. Now, get out!"

"But I only had a mere three plates of rice and beans. Is there a Chinese or Japanese take-out near here?"

Pete grabbed Hector by his ears and said, "Do you have cotton in these ears? No more food! You could get sick! Now, get lost!"

"Not again," said Hector. "We just got back from being lost."

Ann pulled Hector by the hand, and said, "Let's go." She thanked Pete for lunch, and then Ann and Hector walked outside.

"Why did you thank Pete?" asked Hector. "He just boxed my ears, and he was rude! I should have punched him in the nose!"

"I am glad you kept your cool," said Ann. "Pete did box your ears, and he was very rude, but he did give us some rice and beans. I am glad you did not yell at him. It is better to get along than to fight. You don't have to fight every time a dude does or says something stupid."

"I suppose so," said Hector.

Ann gave Hector a kiss. "This kiss is for keeping your cool."

"Your lips are as soft as cotton," said Hector.

"If you keep your cool," said Ann with a smile, "there is more where that came from."

"I think I will stay cool forever!" said Hector. "How about another kiss?"

"Not now," said Ann. "I want to go back to my cabin and complete my sketch of the tent and the log cabin by the lake. I will see you this evening."

"I think I would like to play softball with the boys," said Hector.

"Good," said Ann. "

"OK," said Hector. "I will see you this evening."

Hector walked over to the concrete where the boys were playing softball. On his way over there, Hector let out some gas.

"I think I ate too many beans!" he said to himself.

Word List 19 (–er)

her	camp er	oth er
Pe ter	win ter	moth er
un der	wat er	an oth er
o ver	fast er	No vem ber
ev er	fing er	Sep tem ber
nev er	tem per	Oc to ber
riv er	jerk	won der ful
af ter	Herb	jack et
sis ter	fish er man	gathered
		push o ver

For Reading Only

new	summer	banner
bet ter	December	outfit
soon	away	

Word List 19 (–er)

The Herb

The next day, all the kids packed their things and gathered outside of Pete's cabin under a banner that said, "***Peter Makes the Best Food in Camp!***"

"Best food?" Nat said with a grin. "Peter's food is the *only* food in camp."

The camping trip was over, and the bus would soon come to take them home.

"It was nice to be out of school and away from home for three days in October," said Nat.

"Better here than in school," said Mike.

"You should try camp in the summer," said Jill.

"Yes," Kate added. "It's more fun to be a camper in the summer than camping in the fall or winter. I love to swim in the summer. It feels wonderful to swim in the cool water of a lake on a hot summer day."

"Or to walk across a river with your socks off," added Jill.

"It must be fun to be a fisherman standing in a river with his fishing rod on a summer day," said Nat, "but I have never been a camper in the summer."

"Nat, is this the first time you have ever been to camp?" Kate asked.

Nat looked at her and said, "Yes, Kate, but I would love to come to camp next summer just to see what you and Jill look like in a swim outfit."

"Don't talk like a jerk!" said Jack.

"Sorry," said Nat. "I just think that Kate and Jill must look nice in a swim outfit."

"I don't want you looking at Jill," said Jack. "Not in the summer, not in September, not in October, not in November, not in the winter, not ever! Jill is my girl! You got that, Nat? You stupid little jerk!"

"Nat!" said Hector. "Don't be a Herb! Jack picks on you because he thinks you are a pushover. Don't let him walk all over you!"

"What is he going to do?" asked Jack. "Cry like my little sister?"

"No," said Nat giving Jack the finger. "Like your mother!"

Jack lost his temper and ran after Nat. Nat was faster than Jack, and Jack could not catch Nat. Nat ran to the lake and stopped by a log next to the water. Jack ran to Nat by the lake, and all the other kids ran after them because they wanted to see a fight. Jack jumped at Nat, but Nat ducked. Jack tripped over the log and fell into the water.

"You sure love jumping into the lake," said Nat, "but I think you should get a new swim outfit! Only Herbs go swimming in slacks and a jacket!"

WORD LIST 20 (Contractions)

TWO WORDS	CROSS OUT	CONTRACTION
is not	is n~~ot~~	isn't
did not	did n~~ot~~	didn't
was not	was n~~ot~~	wasn't
are not	are n~~ot~~	aren't
have not	have n~~ot~~	haven't
has not	has n~~ot~~	hasn't
he is	he ~~is~~	he's
it is	it ~~is~~	it's
we are	we ~~are~~	we're
you are	you ~~are~~	you're
they are	they ~~are~~	they're
I am	I ~~am~~	I'm
I will	I ~~will~~	I'll
he will	he ~~will~~	he'll
we will	we ~~will~~	we'll
you will	you ~~will~~	you'll
let us	let ~~us~~	let's
do not	do n~~ot~~	don't
I have	I ~~have~~	I've
we have	we ~~have~~	we've
you have	you ~~have~~	you've
they have	they ~~have~~	they've
could have	could ~~have~~	could've
what is	what ~~is~~	what's
that is	that ~~is~~	that's
you would	you ~~would~~	you'd
he would	he ~~would~~	he'd
cannot	can~~not~~	can't
will not		won't

your — you're
   Is this **your** dog? **You're** a dog!

its — it's
   It's a cute little pup. The big black dog is *its* mother.

there - their — they're
   Look over ***there***.
   Two boys are coming to get ***their*** dog.
   They're running fast.

Word List 20   (Contractions)

I've Had it Up to Here!

"I want you all to sit down on the log!" said Sam. "The bus will be a little late. The man who was going to drive our bus got sick, and they're sending someone new. We've got to talk before we get on the bus."

"Can I go put on some dry things first?" asked Jack, who was still dripping wet from his fall in the lake.

"Make it fast!" snapped Sam. "We're not starting without you."

When Jack came back, Sam said, "I've had it up to here with you kids! We've been at camp for three days, and it's like we're still on the street. What's going on? Jack and Hector had a fight, and they both fell into the lake. Jack can't swim, and he almost died in the water. Hector got mad because of Nat's rap song, so he ran into the woods with Ann. They both almost fell off a cliff, and they lost their way in a dark cave. Now they're glad to be alive, and Ann says she'll never climb a cliff or go into a cave again. If they didn't find a way out just before their light went out, they could've been lost in that cave forever. You'd think that after all this, you kids would stop saying stupid things. But no! A little while ago, Jack snapped all over Nat, and Nat mother-snapped on Jack. Then Jack jumped at Nat and fell into the lake — again! One of these days, Jack will fall into a lake, sink, and never come up! You'd think by now he'd know not to start a fight next to water!

"What's with you kids? When you kids get back on the street, you'll say something stupid to someone with a gun, and that will be the end! Don't you get it? If you keep acting like this, there won't be a next time. You've got to stop all this snapping, if you're going to survive!"

All the kids sat on the log with their lips shut.

"Aren't you going to say something?" asked Sam. "We're not going home until you say something."

"I'll say something," said Jack. "On the street kids snap on me and I snap on them. The street isn't camp. If you don't know how to snap, they'll walk all over you. I'm not going to let any kid walk all over me!"

"The kids said I was a herb, if I didn't snap back at Jack," added Nat. "I wasn't going to stand there and look like a pushover."

"And I can't take it when kids talk about my father," said Hector.

Sam looked at Hector and said; "You'd better find a better way to keep your temper in check. Your mother called me last night. The cops just let your father out, and he wants to see you. He hasn't seen you and you haven't seen him for a long time."

Just then, the bus drove up. "Let's go!" said Sam. "It's time to go home."

WORD LIST 21 (ar, or)

or	art	pa per	art ist
for	cart	rath er	Hec tor
fork	smart	un der	Hec tor's
cork	car	bench	dri ver
pork	far	March	re mark
York	jar	Mars	for get
born	star	stars	for give
corn	yard	yards	for got
worn	hard	corn er	yes ter day
horn	lard	morn ing	im por tant
thorn	cards	darl ing	to geth er
form	farm	farm er	com ple ted
storm	harm	piled	gar den
sort	arm	plan et	de part
short	charm	charm ing	gar ments
sport	part	start	star ted
port	park	base	plas tic
porch	dark	baseball	north west
torch	Mark	inn ing	mor bid
north	shark	tucked	in ter rup ted
Lord	spark	sports ball park	sports man ship

For Reading Only

store	four	words	seat
snore	forty	deep	minutes
stood	letter	new	anything

Word List 21 (ar,or)

A Kiss He Will Never Forget

"Form a line at the bus, kids!" said Sam. "Jack, you take the fifth seat across from me! Hector, make sure to sit in the back, away from Jack! It's a 200 mile trip back to New York, and I don't want any more fights!"

"That's OK," said Jack. "Can Jill sit next to me?"

"Sure," said Sam. "There's no harm in that."

All the kids piled onto the bus. Most of the boys went to the back. Ann took a seat next to Hector. Nat took a seat next to Kate in the front of the bus. The other girls sat together near the boys in the back.

Jack put the wet garments that he had worn when he fell into the lake in a plastic bag. He put the bag under his seat.

Sam stood up at the front of the bus and said, "The bus will depart in four minutes. Make sure you didn't forget anything in your cabin."

"I forgot my art pad!" said Ann. "I just completed my sketch of a cabin by the lake this morning — the one that I had started at the top of the mountain. I think I left it on the cabin porch."

"That was not too smart," said Sam. "Get it fast! The cabin is not too far — only about forty yards away."

Ann wanted to be an artist, and this sketch was very important to her. She jumped off the bus and ran to the cabin. Her art pad was on a bench on the porch. She picked up the art pad, and tucked it under her arm. Mark, the new bus driver, was tapping the horn.

"We've got to get started," said Mark. "I want to get back to New York before it gets dark. A storm is coming from the north or northwest."

"We can't start until Ann gets back," said Sam.

While Ann was running back from the cabin, she tripped on a short tree stump, and fell into a rose garden. She cut her finger on a thorn. Ann ran back to the bus sucking her finger.
No one was looking when Mark took out a short glass jar from a paper bag. The top of the jar had a thin neck with a cork in it. Mark took the cork out, and took a sip of something from the jar, and then started the bus. Mark took another sip and put the jar back in the paper bag. Then he drove the bus out of camp.

Tim was talking to some of the boys at the back of the bus. "The best part of camp is playing sports," he said. "That was a very good softball game we had yesterday. We were winning six to five with two out in the last inning, but there were three men on base. Big Mike hit the ball on a fly to Hector. Hector dropped the ball and lost the game for us, but no one got mad. That was good sportsmanship."

"Hector had a hard night in the cave the day before, and he has a bad temper," said Mike. "No one wanted to start up with him."

"You have to forgive me for dropping the ball," said Hector. "The sun was in my eyes, and I tripped over a rock. I don't like the ballpark at camp. I'd rather play ball in a school yard, or in a park in New York."

"You see," said Mike. "It's a good thing we didn't say anything when he dropped the ball. Even a little remark can spark Hector's temper."

"I didn't like that last remark," said Hector. "I can keep my cool! I can be a good sport! Just watch! When March comes, we'll start playing baseball in the park, again. I will hit the ball hard. If I miss the ball...."

"Not *if*," interrupted Mike. "**When** you miss the ball!"

Hector looked hard at Mike and said, "Shut up, Mike, you big fat lump of pork lard!"

"Very charming, boys!" said Sam. "That's not the sort of sportsmanship we've been talking about!"

"Mike should know not to mess with me!" said Hector. "I was born to snap! If you snap at me, I'll snap back at you like a mad shark."

The bus was going fast. Mark tapped on his horn hard as he passed a car on his left. The bus took a right at a fork in the road next to a farm and sped by a farmer, who was pushing a cart piled up with corn.

The boys in the back of the bus were playing cards. It was getting dark. Sam shut his eyes and began to snore. Nat was in the front seat with Kate. Kate looked outside. "Look at that star!" she said.

"That's not a star," said Nat. "I think it's the planet Mars, but when I'm with you, Kate, I feel like I can fly to the stars."

Kate smiled at Nat. Kate was full of charm. Her eyes were as bright as a torch on a dark night, and Nat loved to see her smile. Nat put his arm around Kate and said, "Darling Kate, I love you." Kate put her lips on Nat's lips and gave him a kiss that he would never forget."

Just then, the bus made a right at a corner and came to a stop next to a store. Mark got out of the bus and went into the store. In about four minutes, he came back to the bus with a paper bag. Mark took out a new glass jar from the bag, pulled out the cork, and took a long drink. Nat saw dark letters on the jar that said, "Fine Port Wine."

"Good Lord!" said Nat. "The bus driver is drinking on the job! He should not drink and drive. He could kill someone!"

"Don't be so morbid my love," Kate said, as she looked deep into Nat's eyes. Nat would never forget Kate's last words on the bus.

WORD LIST 22 (er,ir,ur) [Review: no English word ends with "v": a silent "e" is added to "v" at the end of a word.]

sir	turn	per	start ing
girl	burn	per mit	closed
bird	burnt	per son	Thurs day
dirt	burp	per haps	Sat ur day
birth	curb	per fume	birth day
third	curve	per fect	for ev er
first	curled	nerve	an oth er
shirt	hurt	serve	swim mer
skirt	mur mur	de serve	dif fer ent
chirp	sur prise	swerve	re mem ber
flirt	sur face	lan tern	ham burg er
thirst	dis turb	stern	in ter est ing
con firm	fly ing	ex pert	sub merged
tone	sink ing	long er	ex plo ded
miles	mo ment	bet ter	per man ent
tank	pock et	latch	un der stand
torn	brakes	hap pen	thun der
marks	o pened	hap pened	thun der clap
new born		riv er bank	sub merged

For Reading Only

air	curse
thirteen	through
answer	answered
tried	cried
rain	road
window	fire
hear	heard
head	hour
deeper	holding
roadside	

Word List 22 (er,ir,ur)

Submerged in Water

Mark, the bus driver, stepped on the gas and took another sip of wine. The bus was going 70 miles per hour. Nat was thinking that they should not permit a person like that to drive a bus.

"How can he be an expert driver when he drinks so much?" he said to himself. Nat put on his seat belt, but he did not have the nerve to tell Mark to stop drinking.

Jill was trying to flirt with Jack, but Jack was thinking about Flame. Hector and Ann were talking about a surprise birthday present they were planning to get for Kate. She would be thirteen next Saturday. Ann said she would go shopping on Thursday. Big Mike was in the back seat eating a hamburger that he had saved from yesterday's lunch. Mike took a sip from his third can of coke, let out a burp, and smiled. Mike wished that someone would serve him another hamburger. Sam was starting to snore, again.

Nat closed his eyes and began thinking about Kate. He was thinking that he would always want to remember the taste of Kate's perfect lips and the smell of her perfume. Kate was the first girl that he had ever kissed, and Nat wanted to remember his first kiss forever. He was thinking that this was, perhaps, the best day of his life — even better than the day of his birth. Kate was a very interesting person. She was different from any girl he had ever met, and he did not understand how he came to deserve a girl like Kate. He did not want anything to disturb how good he felt that moment sitting next to Kate on the bus. But things did not turn out that way.

Just then, there was a thunderclap. A spark of lightning lit up the river that ran along the side of the road. It began to rain hard, and there was a lot of wind. Mark took another sip of wine and stepped on the gas. Mark had a very big thirst for wine, and he had a lot more nerve when he was drinking.

The bus began to swerve as Mark drove around a curve at 80 miles per hour. The bus hit a curb and jumped over the side of the road. Mark stepped on the brakes, but he could not stop or turn the bus. The bus made skid marks in the dirt on the roadside, almost hit a tree, and slid down the riverbank. Then the bus hit a rock and flipped over into the cold river water. The gas tank exploded when the bus hit the rock, and the bus began to burn, but the fire went out as soon as the bus hit the water. The back of the bus was sticking out above the water, but the front of the bus was submerged in the river.

When the bus turned over after hitting the rock, Kate went flying into the front window. Her head hit the glass, and she fell back onto the front steps. Mark, the bus driver, pushed the front door open. Water rushed into the bus and pushed Mark back. He tripped over Kate, who was curled up like a newborn baby on the steps by the front door. Mark got up, made his way to the back door, and swam out. The bus driver, saved himself, but the didn't save any of the kids.

"Open the back door of the bus!" yelled Sam, who woke up when the bus began to skid.

"The door is stuck!" yelled Tim.

"Let me try," big Mike said. Mike pulled the latch down, and pushed hard. The door opened, and the kids at the back of the bus began to climb out and swim to the riverbank. Jack could not swim, and he was in the water holding onto the back of the bus. Jill was an expert swimmer. She grabbed Jack by the shirt with one arm, and used her other arm to swim to land.

Sam was trying to find any kids who did not make it out, but it was too dark to see. Sam heard a murmur, but he could not see where it came from. Then there was a flash of lightning, and Sam saw a girl on the floor. It was Ann. He picked her up and took her to the back door. Then he grabbed the back of her shirt and pulled her through the water as he swam to the riverbank.

Nat did not go flying into the front window when the bus flipped over because he had put on his seat belt. He felt for Kate's hand, but she was no longer in her seat.

"Kate! Kate!" Nat called out, but there was no answer. He got out of his seat, and started to feel around for Kate. He felt her cotton skirt, but water rushed in from the front door that Mark had opened. The water pushed Nat back. Nat dived into the water and swam to Kate. He grabbed her hand and tried to pull her out the front door, but the river current pushed Nat's head into the hard door. His hand slipped, and he began to go up to the surface of the river. Sam saw Nat on the surface of the water. He dived into the water, grabbed onto Nat's torn shirt, and pulled him to land.

Nat sat up in the dirt by the riverbank and cried out, "Kate! Kate! Where is Kate?" Then Nat added, "Why do bad things happen to good people?"

Kate was missing, and so was Hector. Ann began to cry. She was thinking that she might never see Hector alive again, that Hector might never again see the morning light, or hear a bird chirp.

When the bus flipped over, Hector hit his head on a pole and fell to the floor. He was out cold. The cold water coming into the bus woke Hector up. He began to climb his way to the back door, but the river current pushed hard on the door and the door closed shut. The bus was sinking deeper into the water. Hector was trapped in the back of the bus — the only place that still had air.

A car stopped short at the side of the road. A man stepped out of the car, lit a lantern, and walked down to the river.

"What happened!" the man asked in a stern tone.

"We were going home from camp, sir," Tim answered. "There was a big storm. We were going fast around a curve. I think the driver was drinking, and he was going too fast. The bus jumped the curb, slid on the dirt at the side of the road, hit a rock, and flipped over into the river. The gas tank exploded when it hit the rock. There was a fire, but the fire went out when the bus hit the water. No one got burnt, but a lot of kids got hurt. Two kids are still missing! I think they're still in the bus, and the bus is filling up with water!"

"Where is Hector!" the man yelled. "Where is Hector!"

Hector was looking out of the back window of the bus. His legs were in the water, but his head was in a pocket of air. He was not sure if he would ever get out alive. Then he saw a man on the river bank with a lantern. The light from the lantern lit up the man's face. Looking through the wet glass window, Hector could not see the face too well, but he was sure he had seen this face a long time ago. He just could not remember where or when.

WORD LIST 23   Open and closed syllables, -tion
1. An open syllable ends with a vowel. The vowel sound is long (go, be).
2. A closed syllable ends with a consonant. The vowel sound is short (got, bet)

pre tend	sec tion	lo cate
re vive	ac tion	lo ca tion
re spond	op tion	ro tate
fal len	mo tion	ro ta tion
ham mer	e mo tion	mo tion less
life less	so lu tion	e vac u ate
gasp ing	ques tion	e vac u a tion
cri sis	ques tions	e val u a tion
doc tors	in jec tion	sit u a tion
cor rect	per fec tion	ed u ca tion
per fect	e lec tric	con sult
hos pit al		con sul ta tion

For Reading Only

knew

ambulance

Word List 23 (open/closed syllables, -tion)

Action in a Crisis

The man with the lantern was at the location where the bus had fallen into the river. He was asking a lot of questions, and he was trying to evaluate the situation. There had been an evacuation of the bus, but Hector was trapped in an air pocket at the back of the bus, and Kate was in the front of the bus submerged in the ice cold water. He did not pretend to know the correct solution, but he knew the situation called for action. This was not the time for crying or for a lot of emotion. There was only one option. He had to try to get Hector out first. It might be too late for Kate.

The man with the lantern went into motion. He ran to his car and took out a hammer. Then he ran back to the river and dived into the cold water. When he got to the bus, he broke the back window with his hammer and helped evacuate Hector from the sinking bus. Hector climbed out of the window and swam to the riverbank. Ann ran to Hector and hugged him tight. She was so full of emotion that she could not stop crying.

The man climbed through the window into the bus. He was trying to find the girl who the kids said was still on the bus. Just then, the bus went into motion. All the rain had made the river current very fast. The bus began to rotate as the man swam under water to the front of the bus to try to locate Kate. By the time he found Kate, the bus had made a complete rotation and began to sink into a deeper section of the river. The man had to go up for air. He grabbed onto Kate's arm, pulled her out the open front door, and swam to the surface. When he got to the surface, the man was gasping for air as he held the motionless girl with one hand.

Nat did not consult anyone when he dived into the water to try to help the man save Kate. This crisis called for action, not for consultation. Nat's dive was a perfect dive, and he swam to perfection. He grabbed Kate's other arm and helped the man pull the motionless girl to the section of the river where all the kids were standing.

Nat put his lips on Kate's lips and puffed air into her windpipe, but she did not respond. Kate was in very bad condition. An ambulance came, and they took the motionless girl to the hospital. Nat did not give up hope.

"Doctors have a lot of education," he said to himself. "Perhaps they can revive her with an injection or an electric shock." Then he asked the question, again, "Why do bad things happen to good people?"

As Nat stood motionless on the riverbank watching the ambulance take Kate to the hospital, Hector looked up at the man who had saved his life. Hector could see his face well now. The man that swam in the river and saved his life was his father.

WORD LIST 24A (ee, ea)
Add an 'e' after 'eez', 'ees' and 'eas' (freeze, ease, please).

see	tea	six teen
tree	sea	nine teen
free	eat	thir teen
three	read	fif teen
deep	beat	week
keep	meat	week end
weep	neat	speed ing
feel	seat	ease
jeep	treat	please
seen	ears	tease
teen	hear	beans
green	year	seats
feed	dear	years
teeth	heal	tears
cheer	meal	tea cup
greet	real	pea nut
sleep	steal	pea nuts
street	mean	beat ing
speed	clean	breath ing
meet	each	beat ings
breeze	least	steal ing
freeze	leave	freez ing
sneeze	beast	leaves
squeeze	cheap	scream
cheese	treat	scream ing

WORD LIST 24B (ai, -ought)

aid	faint	ought
paid	jail	thought
rain	rail	fought
pain	hail	bought
gain	pail	brought
main	mail	care
train	sail	sobs
brain	trail	re turn
chains	saint	ta ken
aim	drain	blank et
claim	mail man	prob lems
air	a fraid	scrub
hair	com plain ing	for est
fair	com plained	but ter
pair	brush	af ford
chair	or der	in mates
wait	din ner	ex pect ing
waist	seemed	rec og nize

For Reading Only

son
easy
since
dead
everyone
once

Word List 24 (ee, ea, ai, -ought)

Jail Years

Hector's father had been in jail for nine years. Hector had not seen his father since he was a little boy, but he could still recognize his father's face.

"Dad?" Hector asked, as he looked at the man in the dim light of the lantern. "Is that you?"

"I thought you wouldn't recognize me," Hector's father said. "It has been so many years. Are you all right?"

Hector's face was green, and he was shivering. His bottom teeth were tapping into his top teeth. "I'm cold," Hector said. "The river water is freezing ...and I'm afraid for the girl who was taken to the hospital. She wasn't breathing. I don't think she was alive when you brought her out of the water. That section of the river was very deep. She had no air."

"Come into my jeep," his father said. "I'll give you a blanket and put on the heat. Then we can talk."

"It's not fair to leave the other kids out here in the rain, while I go into a jeep with heat," complained Hector. The other kids were under a tree with wide green leaves, trying to keep out of the rain.

"I have to talk to you alone," Hector's father said. "You're freezing! Your face is green, and you can't stop shivering! Your friends will have to wait. I can't give each of them a seat in my jeep. You know what I mean? There must be fifteen or sixteen kids out there."

"I don't care if there are nineteen kids out there!" said Hector. "They are my friends. We can all squeeze in! Please! It will be a breeze!" Hector started to sneeze.

"You know you can't squeeze nineteen kids into a jeep!" Hector's father said. "Use your brain, and stop complaining! Get into the jeep before you freeze!"

Hector climbed into the jeep and sat in the front seat. His father went to the back and brought Hector a blanket. He put some hot water in a teacup, put a tea bag into the cup, and gave it to Hector. "Drink some tea," he said, as he started the jeep and put on the heat. "Would you like some meat to eat, and some peanuts? I have some leftover beef that I brought from home."

"I don't feel like having a meal," said Hector, "You don't have to feed me, but did you say you brought this leftover food from *home*? Have you been at home with Mom? And when did you get out of jail? And how did you find our location by the river?"

"Take it easy, Hector," his dad said. "One question at a time, son. I was in jail for nine years. I used to steal from people. I was a mean person. I was mean to your mother. Sometimes I would hit her. I used to drink a lot, and when I got mad I would beat her. I even remember giving *you* a beating when you were just a little kid. You would scream when I hit you, so I would hit you again to shut you up, but that would only make you scream some more.

"Your mother once tried to stop me from hitting you, so I grabbed her by the hair and punched her in the face with the back of my hand. Then she picked up a chair and hit me in the waist. I fought with her so much that she wanted to kick me out of the house. That was not the way a man ought to treat his wife, or his son. The main thing is: I gave too much pain to my dear wife and kid. I was nuts.

"I never had much of an education. I dropped out of high school when I was a teen. My dream was to get a new sports car and to go speeding down the street, but I had no money. I couldn't even afford a new pair of sneakers. The kids on the street used to tease me about my worn out sneakers. So I would go out and steal, but I did not gain anything from stealing. I paid a lot for my stealing. I was always afraid that the cops would catch me. I fought with everyone I loved, and I was not happy. I was all alone. I could not even talk to God.

"One day, I robbed a bank, and the cops came and took me away. When I was sent to jail, they took me on a train in chains. I'll never forget that day. There was thunder, and it started to hail — ice balls from the sky. It seemed like even God was mad at me.

"I felt a lot of shame when they took me away on a train in chains, but that was the least of my problems. I could not stand being locked up like a beast. The jail was not clean, and the food was cheap — peanut butter or dry cheese for lunch. I would not feed that to my dog. I liked real food, like the rice and beans your mother used to make for me. They gave me a pail and a brush, and made me scrub the bathroom. I would go to sleep each night and dream about the outside. I dreamed about being free, about sailing on the sea, or hiking on a green forest trail, but I had to wait and do my time before I could be free again. I would wake up and sit on my bed and weep until there were no tears left. I could hear with my ears the faint sobs of other inmates crying through the night. Nothing could ease the pain. All I could do was wait, day after day, week after week, year after year. My life was down the drain. The only thing that would cheer me was the thought that I would see my son again. It would be neat to greet my son and give him a hug.

"The mailman came each day with the mail, but I never got any. Your mother was so mad at me for beating her that I never got any mail from her. When I called her up to speak to her, she wouldn't answer. I felt all alone. My aim in life was to get out of jail and see my wife and son again. I was afraid that my little son, now a teen, would not remember me. I wanted you to meet me, but I wasn't sure how you would greet me when we met. I never expected that I would have to save you from a sinking bus in order to meet you."

"Dad," said Hector. "When I was in a cave, I had a dream that you could not swim, that you were sinking in the water, and I could not save you. I wanted to come to your aid, but I couldn't. I did not understand the dream, because I knew you were a good swimmer. Ann said that I knew my father could swim in water, but that I was afraid that he could not swim in life. Pop, you swam through the water and saved my life, but can you swim in life? Are you going to go back to stealing and beating people up, and go back to jail?"

"Never, son," said Hector's Dad. "I am a new man, and I want to keep clean. I will never act like that again. I can swim in life, now. I can even help save *your* life."

"Where do you claim to get the jeep, if you just came out of jail?" asked Hector.

"My best friend let me use it for a week. I have to return it to him on the weekend."

"Will Mom let you live with us at home?" asked Hector.

"No, not yet," Hector's Dad said, "but we are speaking to each other. I just had dinner with her at your house. She still makes great beef with rice and beans. But I am living, for now, at my friend's house — the same person who let me use his jeep. I should take you home now."

"We can't!" said Hector. "I cannot leave my friends. I have to know what happened to Kate. We were planning a surprise for her birthday. She is going to be thirteen on Saturday."

"Hector," said his father. "I don't think the girl is alive. She wasn't breathing when I took her out of the water. Her heart was not beating. She was ice cold. She's dead, Hector. She was dead when I took her out of the water."

Hector looked out the window. The rain had stopped, but Nat's tears did not stop. Nat was screaming and crying, "It's not fair! Kate was like a saint! Why did she have to die? Why?"

WORD LIST 25 (-ay, oa) Long 'a' at the end of a word is spelled 'ay' (pay, ray, today)

pay	oak	to day
pain	soak	Sun day
ray	croak	birth day
rain	road	ex tra
play	load	pray er
plain	toad	oat meal
day	moan	sail boat
may	loan	rain coat
say	groan	meat loaf
lay	loaf	Ray mond
bay	boat	forth
jay	coat	meals
clay	goat	bribe
stay	float	loss
pray	throat	church
gray	toast	warm
tray	roast	giv en
sway	boast	sway ing
spray	oath	feelings
a way	roach	re fused
may be	soaked	re mains
	crime	thir teenth

Word List 25 (-ay,-oa)

A Prayer and a Groan

Hector said to his father, "I'm sitting here with you in a warm jeep, while Nat is out in the cold crying about Kate. I cannot stay in here. Maybe I can do or say something to help."

"There is nothing that you can say to make Nat's pain go away," Hector's Dad said. "That's plain to see, but friends should stick together at times like this. I have an extra raincoat in the back seat. Nat must be soaked from the rain."

Hector took the raincoat and a gray blanket, and walked over to the other kids, who were standing under an oak tree next to the road. He handed the coat to Nat, but Nat refused to take it.

"May I have the raincoat?" Ann asked. Ann was shivering from the cold.

"Sure," said Hector, "but it's only a loan. I have to give it back to my father."

"Can we use the blanket?" asked Jack, who was standing next to Jill. Hector put the gray blanket over Jack and Jill's back.

"I think this blanket smells bad," Jack said to Jill.

"Hector!" called Jack. "Your father's blanket stinks. It smells like meatloaf. Are you sure this blanket wasn't used to cover a goat?"

"Shut up, toad brain," Hector said to Jack. "I don't want to boast, but that was the best blanket I could steal from your father's house. You know the house — that big box on the side of the road."

"At least my father's house doesn't have bars on it," said Jack.

Hector was about to punch Jack in his fat lip, but Hector stopped himself. He knew it was stupid to start fighting at a time like this. It was more important to help Nat.

Just then, another bus came to pick the kids up and take them home. As the kids started to climb onto the bus, the cops put Mark in handcuffs. "You are going to jail because you had the nerve to drive a school bus while drinking wine," said a cop. The cop put his hand on the hair of Mark's head, as Mark was put into the cop car at the side of the road.

"I hate you!" Ann yelled at Mark. "Look at what you did to Kate! How could they let a goat like you drive a bus? "

"Oh, shut up, you stupid little kids!" Mark yelled back, as he let out a burp that smelled of wine."

"Say it! Don't spray it!" said Ann.

"I hope you croak, you stinking toad!" added Hector. "I wish I could lay my hands on your throat!"

"If you do that," Dad said to Hector, "then you will end up in jail with Mark. It doesn't pay to play with a roach."

The cop got into the car and drove Mark away.

By now, most of the kids were on the new bus.

"Are you going back home with your father in the jeep, or are you going back with us on the bus?" asked Sam.

"I'm going with my father," said Hector. "Dad, may Ann go with us in the jeep? She's my girlfriend."

"Sure," Hector's dad said. "I didn't know you had a girlfriend."

"Ann," said Hector. "I would like you to meet my father."

"Hello, Ann," Hector's father said. "My name is Raymond. You can call me Ray. Would you like a ride home with us in the jeep?"

"Would you like to come with us?" Hector asked Ann.

"Sure," said Ann, "I don't want to ride on a bus right now, after what happened on the last bus, but what about Nat?" Nat was sitting at the side of the road swaying back and forth like a baby who had lost its mother. They could hear him moaning and groaning. He was in deep pain because of the loss of Kate.

Ann, Hector, and Raymond walked over to Nat. "Would you like to go home with us in my father's jeep?" asked Hector.

"I don't want to go home," said Nat. "I want to see Kate. She must be awake by now."

"She wasn't breathing when I took her out of the ice cold water," Hector's father said. "Her heart stopped beating. I think she's dead."

"No! No! No!" cried Nat. "It can't be! Not my Kate! I wish this day had never come. I wish that stupid bus could float like a boat. I hope they take that bus driver, light up some coal, and roast him in fire. Then they can dump his remains in the bay.

"Why didn't I make Kate put on a seat belt. I put on a seat belt, but I let her remain in the front seat without one. I saw Mark drinking wine. Why didn't I say something? I hate myself! I will never forgive myself."

"Don't beat up on yourself," said Ann. "You didn't kill her. Kate never put on a seat belt when she was in a car or a bus. A lot of us saw Mark drinking, and no one said anything. Don't blame yourself. Some things just happen."

"Why do some things just happen?" said Nat. "Why do bad things happen to good people?"

"I don't think there's a good answer to that," Raymond said. "There are some things that we just can't understand. Maybe some day we will be given the answer. If not in this life, then in the next life. "

"I don't want an answer in the next life," said Nat. "I want to know today!"

"Today, your friends are here for you," Hector's father said. "When bad things happen to good people, friends stick together."

There was a little bit of light in the night sky. It was about fifteen minutes before sunrise.

"Maybe, there's a ray of hope," said Ann, looking at the light coming into the sky. "I heard the man in the ambulance ask for ice. I saw them putting ice and cold water on Kate's head and chest. She was ice cold, when Hector's father took her out of the river. Why were they keeping her cold? If she's dead, why do they want to soak her in ice?"

Nat began to pray. "Please, God, answer my prayer. I am only made of clay. You, who are the giver of life, please give life to Kate. I make this oath today. If you save her life, I will go to church every Sunday. I will set a goal to do well in school. I will not loaf around all night watching TV. I will finish the meals my mother makes for me, even if it is cold oatmeal in the morning, or meatloaf on toast at night. Please, God, I will do anything! Just don't let Kate die!"

"I don't think you can sway God with a bribe," Hector's father said, "but I do hope your prayer is answered."

"I don't think there is a God," said Hector. "When I was little, I prayed every day that I would wake up and find my father in the kitchen drinking tea with my mother, but God did not answer my prayer. I prayed every night, and every morning I would wake up without a father."

"Maybe, God did answer your prayer, but His answer was *No*," Hector's father said. "You can't blame God for my going to jail. I did the crime, and I had to do the time. The answer to your prayer was "No" because I said *No* to the good life. I want to say *Yes* to life now!"

"I hope that the answer to Nat's prayer is *Yes*," said Ann. "I want Kate to see her thirteenth birthday."

"A lot of time the answer to a prayer is *No*," Hector's father said. "Remember, Kate wasn't breathing when I took her out of the cold water."

"Please," said Nat. "Take me to the hospital. I can't go home now. I have to see Kate!"

"Dad," said Hector. "Take us to the hospital. Like you said, *when bad things happen to good people, friends stick together*."

A ray of light was in the sky. It was sunrise, and a blue jay began singing. Hector, Raymond, Ann, and Nat got into the jeep and went down the road to the hospital.

WORD LIST #26A (-y = long /e/, suffix -ly).
Reading rules:
1. 'Y' at the end of a one-syllable word has the sound of long /i / (by, sky).
2. 'Y' at the end of a multisyllable word (following a consonant) usually has the sound of long /e/ (rainy, baby).
3. 'ly' added to a word has the sound of /lee/, and changes the word to an adverb (likely, really, quickly).

by	rainy	mad ly	mess y
baby	greedy	like ly	chill y
try	dusty	soft ly	fuss y
entry	rusty	short ly	smell y
sky	windy	real ly	hur ry
risky	sticky	quick ly	twen ty
sty	bumpy	safe ly	thir ty
misty	sleepy	bad ly	for ty
spy	hairy	frank ly	fif ty
crispy	can dy	glad ly	six ty
my	ug ly	late ly	sev en ty
creamy	ti ny	deep ly	nine ty
arm	story	si lent ly	plen ty
army	fairy	tight ly	nas ty
arms	ti dy	hope ful ly	emp ty
shy	very	care ful ly	filthy
fishy	every	sud den ly	sticky
body	easy	nor mal	brandy
stormy	flim sy	nor mal ly	fing ers
flat	clum sy	fam i ly	sta tion
waves	flim sy	clear	dry ing
park ing	lazy	clear ly	in creased
parked	cheek	seemed	real ized
odds	deeds	wires	ex am ined
	tubes		con nec ted

WORD LIST   #26B

For Reading Only

slow	slowly	friendly
sometimes	brother	hurry
pretty	whole	funny
sunny	Daddy	race
nurse	nurses	hungry
working	oxygen	world
icy		

Word List 26 (y = long e)

Body on Ice

It had been a long stormy night. The sun was coming up, but the air was still chilly. Today would be a sunny day, not like the rainy, windy night that had just passed.

"I feel chilly," said Ann. She was still cold and wet from her swim in the icy river. Hector put his arm around Ann to try to warm her.

"I'll put the heat bacon," Hector's father said. "The jeep should warm up shortly."

The road to the hospital was bumpy and dusty. The jeep could only go twenty to thirty miles per hour. Ann and Hector were sleepy, and they slowly drifted off to sleep. Nat could not sleep. He sat silently in the back of the jeep holding onto the flimsy hope that Kate might still be alive. The air was still misty from the rainy night that had just passed, but the sky was clear now, and the sun was slowly drying things up. After awhile, the road got better. The jeep was going forty to fifty miles per hour. They passed by an army base. An old rusty tank stood motionless near the side of the road.

Raymond stepped on the gas, and the jeep increased its speed to sixty miles per hour. Hector woke up, but Ann was still deeply in sleep. Raymond increased the jeep's speed to seventy miles per hour. "It feels like you're going ninety miles per hour, Daddy!" Hector said. "Please, slow down and drive carefully. I want to get to the hospital safely."

"I would gladly slow down," said Hector's father, "but I thought you kids were in a hurry."

"We *are* in a hurry to get to the hospital," said Hector, "but, frankly, I'm afraid about getting into another crash. That last bus crash was about all I can take."

"I don't think we're likely to get into another crash," Hector's father said. "I'm not drinking any wine or brandy. Drinking and driving is too risky. But I will drive more slowly, if it makes you feel better."

Hector held Ann's hand. Her skin felt soft and creamy. Hector kissed Ann softly on her cheek. Looking at her pretty face, he realized for the first time how madly in love he was with her.

Raymond pulled into a gas station. "My gas tank is almost empty. While I fill up with gas, maybe you kids would like to go inside and get a snack."

"I'm not hungry," said Nat.

Ann woke up, but she was feeling too lazy to get out of the jeep. Hector went inside and came back with four bars of candy. He bit into one of the candy bars, and gave another candy bar to Ann.

"This candy is really crispy." Hector said as he licked his sticky fingers. "A bit messy, but really very good. Nat, Are you sure you don't want one? I'm not greedy. I have plenty of candy."

"I'm really not hungry," said Nat. "I can't eat at a time like this."

Hector had a tiny bit of candy left, but he dropped it on his jeans.

"You really are a clumsy slob," joked Ann. "It's a pity you can't be more tidy."

"It's a pity your tiny nose is pretty ugly," joked Hector.

"What?" asked Ann. "Did you say that my tiny nose is pretty ugly?"

"Oh, no," said Hector. "I said it's a pity ugly girls don't have your pretty tiny nose."

"Oh," said Ann. "I thought so."

Raymond started the jeep, again. They would soon be at the hospital. Ann was rubbing her right eye. "My eye feels itchy," she said.

"Your eye is all red and sticky," said Hector. "I think you have a sty, or pink eye. That eye looks pretty nasty. When we get to the hospital, I want a doctor to look at it."

Soon, they were all at the hospital. The front gate said, "No Entry." Raymond had to go around to the side of the hospital. He quickly parked the jeep in the parking lot, and they all went inside.

Inside, they saw the driver of the ambulance. The ambulance driver was a tall man with very hairy arms. Nat ran over to the man and said, "Kate! Where is Kate? Is she alive How is she? Why did you put ice on her? Is she going to live? How is she?"

"Take it easy," said the man in a friendly tone. "I'll tell you the whole story. When we put Kate into the ambulance, she wasn't breathing. Her heart had stopped beating. If the brain is without oxygen for over four minutes, the person will die. But when the body is ice cold, the brain can survive for an hour. We kept her ice cold, so that we would have a chance to revive her at the hospital. I was not shy. I took a peek into the room where the doctors were working on her, and I tried to spy on what they were doing. The doctors gave her an electric shock to get her heart started, but it didn't work. Then they gave her an injection right into her heart, but that didn't work. Then they gave her another electric shock, and her heart started beating slowly. They connected her blood to some tubes and slowly began to warm up her blood. Hopefully, her brain will be all right, and she will live a normal life."

"Then she's alive?" asked Nat.

"Yes! Kate's alive. Her heart is beating, and she's breathing, but she's still out. She hasn't opened up her eyes yet. They say that her odds of making it are fifty-fifty."

"Can I see her?" asked Nat.

"They will never let you see her the way you look now," said the driver. "The nurses are pretty fussy. You are filthy and smelly from the river. You had better go into the bathroom and wash up, before you try to see her."

Nat washed up and brushed his hair. He walked over to the nurse's station and asked a nurse to see Kate. He told the nurse he was Kate's brother. The nurse looked at Nat like something was fishy, but she let him into Kate's room.

Kate's eyes were shut. Nat sat on a chair next to her bed, and held her hand tightly. Nat thought Kate looked as pretty as a fairy. He bent over and spoke softly in her ear, "Kate, it's me, Nat. I'm so glad to see you. I was so afraid I would never see you again. I'm madly in love with you, Kate. I would gladly give my life for yours. I wish it was me in the hospital, not you. Please, wake up, Kate. Please."

Kate slowly opened her eyes. "Nat, is that you?" she asked softly. "Where am I?"

"It's me," said Nat. "You are in the hospital."

"I had a very funny dream," said Kate. "The dream seemed so real. I was looking down, and I saw myself on a cot with ice all over my body. As I looked down at myself, I felt very good. It was as if I had died, but I wasn't afraid. Doctors were standing around my body. They put some wires on my chest and gave me an electric shock. Then I saw a doctor giving me an injection into my heart. Then he gave me another electric shock. After that, it was like I came back into my body. That was a very funny dream, but it seemed like it was real."

Suddenly, a doctor came into the room. He was surprised to see Kate awake. "How do you feel?" he asked.

"I feel fine," said Kate. "I feel like I have been given a new life. Doctor, did I die and come back?"

"I can't say," said the doctor. "You weren't breathing. Your heart had stopped beating. Your brain waves were flat. We used to say that a person is dead when the heart stops and the brain waves are flat, but now we can sometimes bring a person back. Normally, a brain dies without oxygen after four minutes, but the cold water in the river and the ice saved your brain and your heart."

"Doctor," said Kate. "I had a dream."

"You could not have had a dream," said the doctor. "If you had been dreaming, your brain waves would have been active. Your brain waves were flat."

"Then I wasn't dreaming?" asked Kate. "But you are the doctor who gave me an injection in my heart. I saw you! And you gave me two electric shocks, too!"

"How did you know that?" asked the doctor. "Someone must have told you. Maybe you heard people talking before you woke up."

The doctor quickly examined Kate and walked out of the room.

"Nat," said Kate, "I think I died and came back. In my dream I heard someone say, 'It's not your time, yet. You must go back.' I felt very good looking down at my body, and I didn't want to go back, but then I thought of you, and my family, and then I don't remember any more.

"I know one thing, now. If we do good in this world, we don't have to be afraid to die. I'm going to live every moment of my life, and do all the good deeds I can."

Kate and Nat looked silently into each other's eyes.

Suddenly, Kate's mother and father walked into the room. Kate's mother ran over to Kate saying, "Kate, I was so afraid when I heard what happened to you on the bus. I'm so glad to see you!" Kate's mother kissed her on the cheek and cried.

Kate's father was clearly upset. He looked at Nat and asked Kate, "Who is this boy, Kate?"

"Daddy, this is Nat," said Kate. "He is my friend."

"Please leave the room, Nat," Kate's father said. "I wish to talk to Kate alone."

Nat sadly walked out of the room.

Kate's father sat on Kate's bed and said to her, "I'm so happy you are OK. There is just one thing. Lately, you haven't been telling me about your friends. I don't want you to see this boy any more."

"Why Daddy?" asked Kate. "Nat is a very nice boy. Please don't treat him badly."

"I don't care how nice that boy is!" said Kate's father. "Frankly, I only want you to go out with boys of your own race."

WORD LIST #27 (-old,-ild,-ind, ou, ow = /ou/ or /long o/)
Reading patterns:
1. 'i' and 'o' before a double consonants often have long vowel sounds (find, old).
2. 'ou' (as in out, loud, about), at the beginning or middle of a word or syllable.
3. 'ow' (as in now, cow, power) at the end of a word or syllable.
4. 'ow' followed by an 'l' or an 'n' (as in owl, clown).
5. 'ow' can also have the sound of long /o/ at the end of a word, or before an 'l' or an 'n'. (snow, show, own, bowl, grown).

toe	old	cow	out
tow	cold	how	ouch
low	told	now	couch
slow	sold	vow	grouch
show	gold	plow	slouch
snow	hold	brown	loud
glow	bold	clown	proud
grow	bowl	gown	our
blow	bowling	drown	sour
throw	host	drown ing	house
own	post	owl	mouse
grown	most	growl	cloud
find	al most	howl	clouds
kind	al ways	howls	blouse
mind	bark	crowd	round
blind	sill	al low	sound
blinds	pay ing	pow er	shout
re minds	lay er	pow der	shouted
be hind	a sleep	flow er	spout
child	hall way	flow ers	out side
mild	bliz zard	show er	out fit
wild	puff y	tow el	a bout
snow flake	fi nal ly	drow sy	south
slow ly	cra zy	up town	found
win dow	in sults	down town	ground
blow ing	flor ist	down stairs	a round
snow ing	en tered	ex claimed	trou sers
Kim	up stairs	dis gust ing	at ten tion
flakes	ex plain	a part ment	

WORD LIST #27B

For Reading Only

building
robber
wedding
e lev a tor
eye brow
covered
thousand
ex-con
asked

Word List 27 (-old, -ild, -ind, ou, ow = /ou/ or /long o/)

A Mouse in the House

Kate had to stay in the hospital for two more days. Hector's father drove Nat and Ann home, and then he took Hector back to Hector's house. It was a cold day. The sun slid behind a white puffy cloud. Soon the clouds became thick and dark. A snowflake landed on the front window of the jeep. Then it began to snow hard. Raymond parked the jeep around the corner from Hector's house.

"Dad," Hector asked, "when we get home, could you call a florist to send flowers to Kate in the hospital?"

"I am proud of you, son," said Raymond. "You are a good friend. I would love to send Kate flowers, but I am not made out of gold. I don't have any money I can't even send her one flower. The florist will not trust me to lend me any money because I just got out of jail. I have to find a job, and it is not easy for an ex-con to find a job."

"But you are driving a jeep."

"I told you a thousand times, I have to return the jeep to my friend on the weekend I can't afford my own jeep, or even an old used car."

"I don't care if you don't have any money, Pop, just as long as you come home and hold mom's hand."

"Hector, I can't go home with you now. Your mother is still upset with me because of the wild way I behaved in the past. I acted like a stupid clown. She will not allow me to stay in the house, at least for now. I have to go slow with your mother."

"Can you at least come upstairs for awhile?" asked Hector. "I need you to explain to Mom what happened at the river."

"OK," Hector's dad said. "That will give me an excuse to see your mother again. It will be good to be together with my wife and child."

It was snowing hard when Hector and his dad stepped out of the jeep. The mild wind that had been blowing from the south began to blow cold air from the north, but Hector did not mind the snow or the cold blowing wind. It would be the first time in many years that he would be together with both his father and mother. The cars and the lamp post on the corner already had a thin layer of white powder. Hector looked up at the third floor window of his house. The brown plastic owl on the window sill now had a thin layer of white snow. The blinds behind the window were shut.

Hector and his father entered the apartment house. The building was as tall as a tower. Hector was glad that he lived on a low floor because the power to the elevator in his building was not always on. A dog on the first floor began to bark and to growl as they passed by the dark hallway and climbed the stairs to Hector's third floor apartment.

When they got to the apartment, Hector's father tapped on the door. Hector's mother, Kim, slowly opened the door. When she saw Hector standing there she gave him a big hug.

"I was so afraid that something happened to you!" she said. Then she looked up at Hector's father, and a scowl came over her face. "Ray, I thought I told you never to come to my door. How can you be so bold to come up to my apartment? I let you have dinner with me one time to talk about Hector, but I made a vow never to let you into my house again. Now, go back downstairs. Three is a crowd! Why don't you go bowling with your friends and leave us all alone like you used to!"

"Hello, Kim," said Raymond, not paying any attention to his wife's insults. "That's a pretty outfit you have on. I love your blouse. It reminds me of how pretty you looked in your wedding gown."

"Don't try to suck up to me, Raymond," said Kim. "Today you're telling me how pretty I look. The last thing I remember you telling me nine years ago was that I looked like a cow. You would sit next to me on our brown couch and say, '*How about now my little cow* !' You acted like a disgusting pig!"

"Please, don't frown and make such a sour face. I have to explain what happened to Hector. It's snowing hard outside. Please, let me come in and explain."

"Is it really snowing outside?" Hector's mother asked. "I didn't know. My window blinds are shut. Oh, well. You can come in, but just to explain what happened to Hector."

Hector's mother sat on the couch, and his father sat on a brown chair.

"Look at you, Hector!" his mother said. "You are a filthy mess. You look like you jumped in a lake with your shirt and trousers on."

"Not in a lake," Raymond said. "He was in a river."

"What!" she exclaimed. "Hector was swimming in a river at the end of November? Are you crazy, Hector? Go get a towel and take a hot shower. I don't want to see you until you wash yourself and put on a clean pair of trousers and a clean shirt!"

Hector went into the shower, and turned on the water spout. His mother and father were left alone talking in the living room.

Raymond told Kim about how he had saved Hector and Kate from drowning in the river, and how Kate had come back to life after her heart had stopped.

Kim looked at Raymond and said, "You mean our son was about to drown, and you saved his life? And this girl died and came back to life? Wow! Did you make up this story to get on my good side? How low can you get! You were never here to see our son grow! And now that he's almost grown, you show up one day and say you saved his life? Do you think I'm blind? That is the most stupid lie I have ever heard! You say you saved Hector and Kate from drowning in a bus that crashed into a river? Is that what you're telling me?"

"That's what I'm telling you," said Raymond. "Don't be such a grouch. Ask our son, when he comes out of the shower."

Just then, Kim heard a sound. Something small ran under the couch and along side the living room wall. Then Kim let out a loud shout. "A mouse! A mouse!" she shouted. "There's a mouse in the house!"

"I'll set up a mouse trap," said Raymond. "I assure you, the mouse will be dead in the trap by morning."

"But I'm afraid of that mouse," said Kim. "Who is going to throw the dead mouse out in the morning?" Kim was beginning to panic.

"If you let me stay over," Raymond said, "I'll take care of the mouse."

Kim lifted one eyebrow and said, "No way! I made a vow never to let you in my house again. I let you in to tell me about what happened at the river, and now you want to sleep over!"

Hector came out of the shower with a towel around his waist. Raymond walked over to the window and pulled up the blinds. He looked outside the window at the snow. The ground was covered with white powder. He did not have to open the window to hear the howl of the wind. "From the sound of it, this looks like a pretty big snow storm," said Ray. "There is no way I can get my jeep downtown to my friend's house until the snow stops and they plow the street."

Kim looked like she was about to blow up. "Well, you can't stay here!" she shouted. "I told you a thousand times — you can't stay here!"

"Please, mom," said Hector. "Pop just saved my life. You can't send him out in a blizzard. Be a kind host, and don't throw my father out in a freezing blizzard."

"Come over here, Hector, and don't slouch" Hector's mother said. "Tell me. Did your father save you and Kate from drowning in a river?"

"Yes, Mom," said Hector. "Pop saved me and Kate from drowning. The bus was filling up with water, and Dad saved us!"

"Please, Kim," said Raymond. "I am not asking you to forgive me for all the pain I have given you. All I am asking is to let me stay just one night in the same house with my wife and son."

Just then, the mouse ran by again Kim jumped up and hit her toe on the leg of the couch. "Ouch!" she said. "Well, only if you catch the mouse and throw it out in the morning! You can sleep on the couch."

"Yes!" exclaimed Hector with a glow in his eyes.

Hector was feeling drowsy. He went to his room and was soon fast asleep. Hector dreamed of his father swimming in the water It was so different from the dream he once had of his father drowning.

The next morning, Hector woke up and found his father drinking tea with his mother. "God has finally answered my prayer," Hector said to himself.

"Good morning, Dad! Good morning Mom! Isn't it a wonderful morning!"

Hector went into the kitchen and fixed himself a bowl of corn flakes. Never did a bowl of corn flakes taste as good to Hector as it did that morning.

WORD LIST #28A (-oy,-oi,-aw, -au, c=/s/)

Reading rules:
1. 'oy' at the end of a word or syllable (boy, joyful).
2. 'oi' at the beginning or middle of a word or syllable (oil, coin).
3. 'aw' at the end of a word or syllable (saw, lawyer).
4. 'au' (August, haul).
5. c = /s/ when followed by an 'e', 'i', or 'y' (city, nice, fancy). c = /k/ all other times.

boy	oil	saw	Au gust
toy	boil	jaw	pause
soy	foil	law	cause
joy	soil	draw	be cause
en joy	spoil	draw ing	haul
joy ful	broil	straw	vault
foy er	join	see saw	fault
roy al	coin	law	haunt
busboy	coins	law yer	fraud
oy ster	joint	out law	laun dry
an noy	point	aw ful	laun dro mat
annoying	pointed	lawn	au to mat ic
des troy	noise	yawn	caught
sup port	voice	dawn	cau tion
city	choice	crawl	di no saur
cent	re joice	lou sy	res tau rant
cen ter	moist	waiter	sauce
since	a void	treat	sau cer
ac cept	toi let	men u	dec or a tions
add	tur moil	men tion	treatment
fact	sir loin	load ed	em ployed
ov en	a greed	French	em ploy ment
lem on	sub way	dis count	a lu min um
ketch up			ex cel lent

For Reading Only

juice	disappear
once	tomorrow
busy	arrived
clothing	arrived
wood	table
appoint	disappoint

Word List 28   (oy, oi, aw, au, c=/s/)

Busboy at a Restaurant

Hector was full of joy when he sat down in the kitchen next to his mother and father.

"This is the answer to the prayer that I had as a little boy," said Hector. "I have always prayed for the day when I would wake up and find my father in the kitchen drinking tea with my mother."

"Hector," said his father. "I don't want to disappoint you and spoil this joyful morning, but your mother has made up her mind. I was the cause of too much pain in the past, and she does not want me to live here. The time is not ripe for that. She has agreed to see me again, but not in the house. It is too soon for us to get back together. I just got out of the joint last week."

"But Mom, please don't disappoint me. I want us to be a family."

"We are still a family, Hector," his mother said. "We just are not all living in the same house."

Hector's father added, "I have to find employment first. I don't have a cent. I need a job. I don't want to stay in the house, while your mother goes off to work to support you and me. I could not stand that. I saw an add for a job as a busboy in a restaurant in the city It's not a great job, and it's not automatic that I can get it, but I'm going to call and give it a try."

"What is a busboy?" asked Hector.

"Haven't you ever been to a restaurant?" asked his father.

"Ray, did you ever take him to a restaurant when he was growing up?" Kim asked.

"I suppose not," said Ray. "I was a bad father. I was too busy being an outlaw. I did not enjoy my life. My life was in the toilet. When the law finally caught up with me and sent me to jail, I wanted to blame my lousy lawyer, but I finally realized that I was the only one at fault. While in jail, I made this toy dinosaur out of wood for my boy." Ray reached into his bag and gave the toy to Hector. "You're too old for this, now, but I would like you to have it."

Hector's eyes were moist with tears, "Thank you, Daddy. I didn't know you were even thinking about me. Do you have to go? It's very annoying to have you with us one day, and gone the next. The thought of you walking out of my life again makes me boil inside."

"I know it's annoying," said Hector's mother, "and I hate to destroy your joy, but it would be a fraud to pretend that I was still in love with your father. You cannot avoid that fact."

"I would love to get back with your mother," said Hector's father, "but she won't take me back. Not now, even if I crawl back. I am sorry our little family is in such turmoil."

Raymond said goodbye to his son in the foyer, and then Hector's father walked out the door.

"Ray, Drive with caution," Kim shouted, as her husband went downstairs. Then Hector ran to the window and watched his father walk in the snow. Hector saw his father pause for a moment, and then disappear around the corner.

"Hector!" his mother called. "We have to do a laundry! You have a lot of dirty clothing from your trip that is beginning to smell awful. Please, take the laundry to the laundromat and wash your clothing."

"Please don't annoy me with doing the laundry," Hector said with a yawn. "I am sleepy because I woke up at dawn. I want to take a nap. When I wake up, I have to meet Ann in the park by the seesaw. She asked me to join her for a picnic on the lawn. And then Ann wants to draw with me."

"It's not August, Hector!" said his mother. "It's the end of November, and there is snow on the ground! What you said is a fraud! You're not going on any picnic with Ann, and you are awful at drawing! Now, go get the laundry and haul it to the laundromat, before I do something awful to you!"

"Sorry, Mom," said Hector. "I don't have a coin for the Laundromat. I'll do it tomorrow."

"That's the last straw! You are doing the laundry today! Here are some coins. Now go do the laundry and get all that dirty soil out of your clothing, before I hit you up side your jaw! One more thing. While the laundry is drying, go to the grocery store and pick up some milk and juice."

The next day, Hector's mother got a call from Hector's father.

"Don't applaud," she said, "but your father got that job as a busboy at a restaurant in the city. He has invited us to join him at the restaurant on Sunday, on his day off. He gets a discount because he is employed at the restaurant."

Hector could hardly wait until Sunday. When Sunday finally arrived, Hector and his mother took the subway downtown to the restaurant.

When they got to the restaurant and walked inside, Hector said, "Wow!" as he pointed to the decorations on the wall. "Take a look at this joint! Look at all those cool decorations! People who eat in here must be loaded with money!"

"Don't talk so loud," said Hector's mother, "and don't point! This is a very fancy restaurant. You should not make so much noise."

Hector's father was waiting inside. "I don't care how loud Hector's voice is," Raymond said joyfully. "I rejoice each time I hear the voice of my wife and son. Please, come sit down."

"This is a nice joint," Hector said to his father. They all sat down at a table in the center of the restaurant.

"Don't mention the word 'joint'," his father said. "They called our jail house 'the joint'. I would like to forget that awful place."

A waiter in a white shirt and a black tie walked over to their table and handed each of them a menu. "Give my family the royal treatment," Raymond said to the waiter.

"We have very good oysters, served on a bed of brown rice with soy sauce. Perhaps you would like our sirloin of beef, broiled to perfection, served with baked potato. If you like, we have wonderful fish. We can fry the fish in lemon and oil. If you want less fat, we can broil your fish in the oven without oil in aluminum foil."

"I'll have the oysters in brown rice and soy sauce," said Kim.

"Excellent choice," said the waiter.

"I'll have the fish fried in lemon and oil, with a boiled potato." said Ray.

"Excellent choice," said the waiter.

"And I'll have the sirloin of beef with some French fries, ketchup, and a coke," said Hector. "And don't forget the straw!"

After the main meal, they were served tea in a fancy cup and saucer.

"Where did you get the money to pay for all this, Pop?" Hector asked. "Did you rob the vault?"

"Don't play with me," Hector's father said. "Since I work here, I can have dinner here with my family at a big discount."

"Sorry, Pop," said Hector. "I was only kidding."

It was time to leave, so Hector asked the question that everyone seemed to be trying to avoid. "Dad, will you come home and live with me and Mom? Now that you have found employment, you can help pay the bills."

Raymond looked at his son and said, "The choice is up to your mother."

"Hector, darling," Hector's mother said. "It is too soon. I can't forget the past. You will have to accept the fact that we are not going to live together as a family. You will see your father when he comes to visit, or you can spend a weekend with him, but he is not coming home to stay."

Hector was silent. His eyes became moist, and he began to shake. Then he got up and ran out of the restaurant.

WORD LIST 29 (-ong, -ung, -unk)

sing	sang	sung	song
ring	rang	lungs	long
spring	sprang	swung	strong
bring	gang	stung	songs
sink	sank	sunk	a long
drink	drank	junk	long er
stink	stank	drunk	honk
new	spank	stunk	se cret
few	beer	skunk	en joy ing
chew	cream	truck	warm er
grew	sweet	struck	meet ings
stew	raise	shiv er	pro mo tion
		yel low	

For Reading Only

knew
wrong
learn
months
weather

Word List 29 (-ong, -ung, -unk)

Nat's New Rap Song

A few months passed by, and it was the beginning of spring. The air grew warmer, and the birds were singing their songs.

Kate was no longer in the hospital. Her heart and lungs were fine, and she went back to a normal life. She could see Nat at school, or when the gang got together in the street, but her father would not let her go out with Nat. Sometimes she would meet Nat in the park in secret, and they would take long walks together hand in hand. All the kids thought that Kate's father was wrong, but Kate didn't want to get her father mad. Sometimes her father would get so drunk that he would throw up in the sink. Then he would go back and drink some more. At times like this, he was a drunk that stunk like a skunk.

Kate was too old for her father to spank her, but once, when she asked to go out with Nat, her father struck her in the face with the back of his hand. Her father was very strong, and when he struck her, it felt like she got stung by a truck. Kate was a sweet kid, and as long as her father did not know about her secret meetings with Nat, her father did not get mad at her.

Hector's father got a promotion from a busboy to a waiter. He made good money at his new job. The rich people that came to that fancy restaurant left good tips. Hector and his mother ate a few times with Ray at the restaurant. Hector loved to chew on the beef stew.

One spring day, Hector and Ann met Nat and Kate at the park. Nat sang a new rap song he had made up.

If you want to sing along, come on down and hear my song.
I'll tell you how to live your life, to raise your kids and treat your wife.
To be a father or a mother, you must learn to love each other.
Don't drink beer, and don't eat junk, don't become a stinking drunk.
Remember that time when the bus sank in the river,
It was all so very cold, and the kids began to shiver,
I knew I was sunk, and all that junk,
But a man sprang from his jeep, and he swung a big hammer,
He broke the glass, and saved a sister and a brother.
And we all made it home to give a hug to our mother
And now here we all are, all of us together,
Sitting in the park, enjoying spring weather!

Nat had just sung his song, when they all heard an ice cream truck honk its horn and ring its bell. The ice cream man rang the bell again, and then the gang ran to the truck to get some ice cream.

Nat's song made Hector think of his father. Hector was proud of his father. They would not all be here alive and together, if his father had not saved them on the bus.

WORD LIST 30 (Suffixes: -es,-est,-ful,-less,-ment,-ness,–en=/in/)

boxes	thank ful	o pen
inches	wish ful	to ken
punches	harm ful	spok en
benches	hand ful	eat en
kisses	cup ful	beat en
dances	care ful	fro zen
matches	end less	tight en
dresses	help less	fright en
stitches	base less	chil dren
scratches	harm less	mad ness
fast est	strap less	sick ness
slow est	back less	weak ness
soft est	spine less	sharp ly
long est	base ment	part y
short est	pave ment	dress y
strong est	a part ment	ang ry
smart est	de part ment	cra zy
dates	a gree ment	jack ets
race	treat ment	va ca tion
teams	pun ish ment	hope ful ly
showed	a muse ment	Hal lo ween
sec ond	a maze ment	

For Reading Only

hatred
worse
skinny
overheard
instead

Word List 30 (suffixes: -es,-est,-ful,-less,-en,-ment,-ness.)

The Agreement

June came quickly, and summer vacation was only a handful of days off. A few days before the end of school, all the kids met by the benches in the park.

"Didn't this year go fast?" asked Hector.

"It sure did!" answered Ann. "This has been the fastest year ever!"

"For me, this has been the slowest year ever," said Kate. "I can't wait until my father lets me date Nat in the open. Maybe my father will end this baseless race hatred and let me go out with Nat."

"I think that's wishful thinking," said Ann. "Your father will never give up on this madness, but cheer up. You should be thankful that you can still meet Nat at school and in the park. You and Nat can go to the end term dance without dates. Then you can dance with Nat, and your father will never know. This way, you can avoid punishment."

"I'm going to save all my dances for Nat," said Kim.

"And I'm going to save all my kisses for Hector," said Ann.

"I can go for that!" said Hector. "I'm in complete agreement. Ann's kisses are the longest, and her lips are the softest from all the girls that have ever kissed me."

"What other girls?!!" Ann asked sharply. "If you keep making things up, you will end up with endless punches instead of endless kisses. Then your friends will have to pick up your helpless body from off the pavement. Remember, Ann with the softest kiss has the strongest punch!"

"Take it easy," said Hector. "I was only kidding. You're the first and only girl that has ever kissed me."

"I thought so!" said Ann.

The next evening, the whole gang was at the dance. The girls had on pretty dresses, and the boys wore dressy jackets.

To everyone's amazement, Flame showed up in a short, strapless, backless, dress. Jack and all the boys could not keep their eyes off of Flame.

"That's the shortest, backless, strapless dress I have ever seen on a girl outside of forty-second street," said Jill, who was holding a cupful of punch.

"Now wait a second!" said Flame, who had overheard Jill's remark. "Do you have something against short, backless, strapless dresses?"

"No," said Jill. "On you, backless and strapless matches very well with brainless."

"This is not Halloween!" Flame said to Jill. "Be careful. Your dress might frighten the children!"

"If you tighten that dress another inch," Jill said, "the stitches will snap! Where did you get it — from the trash in the basement?"

"I got my dress at a department Store," said Flame. "At least I have the inches to fill my dress, you spineless mouse! You are as skinny as a frozen ice stick after all the ice has been eaten."

"Go get a token and take the subway back to your house," said Jill. "Someone might steal the boxes!"

Flame jumped on Jill and started pulling Jill's hair.

"Watch out!" yelled Jack. "She's not harmless! If she scratches you, you will have to get stitches!" Jack stood there watching hopefully. "I hope the stitches on her dress snap," he thought to himself.

"This is madness!" said Hector. "Dances are for fun, not for fighting. Let's pull them apart!"

Everyone was in agreement with the words that Hector had spoken.

"All this snapping is a sickness," said Nat. "We think we are big and strong when we snap, but it's really a weakness. You have to be strong to know how to talk things out to avoid a fight, or to walk away, if you have to."

"Yes," added Hector. "The smartest thing for a kid to know is how to let someone know how you feel without getting him or her angry. If the situation is too hot, or the other dude is acting crazy, just walk away."

"Are you saying I have a weakness because I like to snap all the time?" asked Jack.

"All this snapping is not harmless," said Ann. "One of these days you are going to snap on the wrong dude, and you will get beaten up, or worse."

"But snapping can be fun!" said Jack.

"Jack's right," said Hector. "Some snaps are very funny."

"But they can be harmful," said Nat "They can hurt people's feelings. Some kids can't take the treatment, and they get angry and start fighting."

"Why don't we have a snapping contest?" asked Ann. "We could have teams! We won't snap at each other, so no one will get mad! Each team will just trade snaps. We'll do it for amusement."

"You're on!" said Jack. "We will have a snapping party at my apartment. The whole gang is invited."

"I don't think we can all fit in those boxes on the street you call your apartment," said Hector.

"Stop kidding around," said Jack. "Save it for the party!"

WORD LIST 31 (Silent 'e', double consonants)
1. When a word ends in silent 'e', drop the 'e' before adding another vowel. (make > making)
2. If a one-syllable short vowel word ends with a single consonant, double the consonant before adding another vowel (get > getting; bet > better).

get ting	make	coming	treat ing
bet ter	making	having	drift
snap ping	take	in hale	po lite
shut ting	taking	in haling	de bate
hap pen	smoke	ex hale	es cape
rot ten	smoking	ex haling	dic tate
mom ma	in vite	lo cate	rep tile
put ting	in viting	lo cating	dis liked
weak	in vited	ed u cate	im po lite
	de cide	ed u ca tion	ad vice
	de ciding	lo ca tion	con fined
	ig nite	spoke	e lec tion
	ig niting	spoken	re mind ed
	ig nited		
	ig nites		

For Reading Only

girlfriends
cigarette
enough
breath

Word List 31 (Silent 'e', double consonants)

Smoking Jill

Jack was upset with Jill. He was not inviting her to his snapping party. Jack said to Jill, "You are not getting an invitation to my party. Stay out!"

Jill was upset at Jack. She disliked the way Jack had spoken to her. She said, "Jack, you are not polite. Didn't your momma educate you better than that?" Jill turned around and went to talk to her girlfriends.

Mike spoke to Jack, "It is a mistake not to invite Jill to your party. I know you dislike her *now*, but you used to like her a lot. Why are you treating her like a reptile?"

"Don't dictate to me who I can invite or cannot invite to my party. We are not debating or having an election. It's my party, and I decide who is invited. Jill is out!"

"I know we are not having a debate about this, and you are the one who is deciding who is coming to your party, but why aren't you inviting your own girlfriend?"

"I don't want to see her again, unless she stops smoking. I like Jill a lot, but I get angry when I see her igniting a match or taking a puff of a smelly cigarette. Its not good for her to inhale that stuff, and she smells bad when she exhales. I don't want to be confined in the same room with her when she is smoking. The smoke makes the room smell. Do you get my drift, Mike?"

"Maybe you should talk to her," said Mike. "Don't make a big mistake by shutting her out. Take my advice. Talk to her!" Mike walked away and went back to his apartment house.

Jack called Jill, who was talking to Ann at the corner. Jill walked over to Jack and said, "What do you want?"

"I want to talk to you," said Jack.

"Why should I talk to you when you are so impolite?"

Jill looked inside her bag to locate a match. She wanted to smoke. She ignited a match and started smoking.

Jack said, "We have been together for a long time. I like you a lot, but I dislike it when you smoke. When you ignite a match, I get upset. If you inhale smoke, you will get sick. My father died from smoking. I do not want anything to happen to you. I really would like you to come to the party, but I also want you to quit smoking."

Jill was inhaling and exhaling the smoke from her cigarette

"I don't want to be impolite," said Jack, "but that stuff really smells nasty. You think a cigarette makes you look cool, but all it does is make your breath smell, and it can make you very sick. You have got to stop smoking! I don't want you to get sick and die like my father did! Do you understand what I'm saying?"

"If you want me at the party, why did you invite Flame?" Jill asked. "I hear she doesn't have to light a cigarette to smoke; all she has to do is light up her stinking breath."

"Save the snaps for the party," said Jack. "I only like looking at Flame, but she is not for me. You are the only girl for me! I want you to come to the snapping party, but only if you vow to stop smoking."

"I did not know that you hate smoking so much," said Jill, putting out her cigarette. "This has been an education. I will try to stop smoking. I hope I can escape from this rotten habit."

"Thanks for hearing me out," said Jack. It was a mistake not to invite you. It's just that your smoking was making me crazy. It reminded me of how my father died. Before he passed away, he got very sick. His lungs were not getting enough oxygen. He was so weak, he could hardly walk. I don't want you to ever get sick like that!"

"Now I understand why you hate smoking so much," said Jill.

"I really would like you to come to the party," said Jack. "It wouldn't be fun without you. Do you know the location?"

"Yes," Jill said smiling. "I will have no problem locating your house. I will see you there."

WORD LIST #32 (oo, ou, ui)

do	took	you	suit
to	cook	youth	fruit
too	foot	soup	swim suit
zoo	good	group	cruise
moo	wood	coup on	screw ball
boo	hood	fir	con tin ue
soon	look	stirs	cho sen
spoon	looked	lock er	al lowed
stoop	wool en	bus pass	parents
poor	bare foot	nickel	re fresh ments
goof			
room			
broom			
snooze			
moose			
loose			
baboon			
sham poo			

Word List 32 (oo,ou,ui)

Good Snaps, Poor Snaps

    The whole gang of kids was at Jack's apartment for the snapping party. A group of kids were chosen for each team. Hector, Ann, Mike, and Flame were on one team. Jack, Jill, Tim and Bill were on the other. They decided to go back and forth, until everyone in the group had a turn. Nat and Kate would decide which team had the best snaps.

    Bill was up first: "When you were born, you looked like a cow. When the doctor slapped you on the butt, you said 'Moo!'"

    "Boo!" said Kate. "That was a poor snap. Mike, you are up now. Let's see if you can do better."

    "When you were born," said Mike, "your parents couldn't find you in the hospital. The doctor said 'Sorry, we sent the moose to the zoo.'"

    "A little better," said Nat. "Your turn, Tim."

    "I heard your sister loves Halloween," said Tim. "That's the only time she is allowed to ride on her mother's broom."

    "Good one!" said Kate.

    "My turn," said Ann. "Your father is such a screwball, in the last snow storm he used a spoon to dig out his car."

    "I liked that one," said Nat. "Your turn, Jill."

    "I heard you were very upset when you could not wash your hair," said Jill. "The store was all out of baboon shampoo."

    "Boo!" said Nat. "Save that snap for the moon. Flame, you're up."

    "Your mother is such a fruit," said Flame, "she goes to work in a loose swimsuit and a fir hood."

    "You're so short," said Jack, "you play handball off the stoop."

    "Your father is so cheap," said Hector, "for his honeymoon, he took your mother on a cruise — in a bathtub."

"Your father is so cheap, he uses a coupon to try to get six cents for a nickel," said Bill. "He dresses like a youth so he can use your bus pass."

"Snaps like that can make a body snooze," said Kate. "Mike's turn."

"You're such a stupid goof ball," said Mike, "when you walked into the girl's locker room, you told the girls to close their eyes."

"Snooze time is coming soon," said Nat. "Who can do better than that?"

"I can," said Tim. "Your mother is such a poor cook, she stirs her soup with the woolen sock from her smelly foot. Your father yelled at her. He told her to take her smelly sock off and stir the soup barefoot."

"Good snap!" said Nat. "We will continue after refreshments."

WORD LIST 33   (Silent letters)

who	write	often	phone
what	wrong	soften	pho ny
when	wrote	listen	tro phy
where	wrist	hour	pho to
why	know	honest	pho to graph
white	knee	ex hib it	tel e phone
whale	knife	bomb	el e phant
whipped	knocked	thumb	al pha bet
whiff	news	climb	graph
wheth er	soda	dumb	half
whisk ers	count	crumb	slammed
whack	icing	dumb est	Car vel
what's			ac cord ing

For Reading Only

break
whose
somewhere

Word List 33 (Silent Letters)

A Trophy for the Dumbest Snap

    The kids took a half hour for refreshments. They had ice cream with whipped cream, and a Carvel Whale Cake with white icing. There was also some nice crumb cake, and they could fill up with soda as often as they liked.
    Big Mike took half a crumb cake, while putting his thumb in the Carvel ice cream cake.
    "Mike! Don't put your thumb in the Carvel Whale Cake," said Nat. "That's dumb. Cut it with a knife, and eat it with a spoon or a fork."
    The telephone rang. Jack picked up the phone.
    "Who is it?" asked Jack. "Hector, it's for you. It's your father."
    Jack handed Hector the telephone.
    "Hello," said Hector. "What's up?...What?...You can't see me this weekend? Why not?...Where are you going?...Who are you going with?... When?... You have to go somewhere with your new girlfriend this weekend?... Why?... Listen, Pop. I don't care whether she's nice or not. It's wrong! What about Mom? I want us to be a family.... What?... I know you are being honest with me, and you are not giving me some phony excuse, but I don't need another mother! That's whack!"
    Hector lifted his wrist and slammed the phone down hard. The phone fell, and it knocked into Hector's knee. Hector's knee did not hurt as much as his feelings. The news about his father's new girlfriend hit Hector like a bomb. Hector's father and mother were not getting back together. There was nothing that Ann could say to Hector that would soften the blow.
    "Time to get back to the snapping contest!" shouted Kate. "There is a small trophy for the dumbest snap, and a big trophy for the best snap."
    "How many elephants fit into a car?" asked Ann. "If you want to know, just count your family the next time they climb out of a car."
    "Good start," said Kate. "Jill is up next."
    "You're so dumb," said Jill, "you get upset because you can't write the alphabet. You can't understand why your thumb is always out of ink."
    "This photograph of your girlfriend is rated 'R'," said Jack. "The photo is so ugly, it might frighten a child under sixteen."
    "According to the list that I wrote," said Nat, "Jack went out of turn. Flame, you go next."
    "Your ugly girlfriend says you stink so much that she wants to break up with you," said Flame. "One whiff of your armpit, and her whiskers fall out!"
    "Flame lit the fire with that snap!" said Nat. "Let's take a break!"

WORD LIST 34 (-le)

lit tle	ap ple	rid dle	ta ble
bat tle	sam ple	can dle	a ble
bot tle	sim ple	pud dle	un a ble
set tle	ma ple	bub ble	la ble
daz zle	pim ple	mid dle	mar ble
daz zled	dim ple	han dle	trem ble
driz zles	crip ple	sad dle	drib ble
snif fle	ex am ple	cud dled	kiss able
ti tle	gig gle	cra dle	lov able
mood	bu gle	poo dle	a dor able
lone ly	jungle	spark le	com fort able
mine	gar gle	tick le	mis er able
hoped	single	pick le	prob ably
rides	gog gles	chuck le	hor rible
book	strug gle	freck le	ter rible
page	snug gling	blew	sen sible
rocked	ten der		pos sible
mouth	fol low		im pos sible
mem bers	re turned		con ver tible

For Reading Only

incredible
label
trouble
control
change
rainwater
change
worry
whose
married
changing
practice

Word List 34 (-le)

Feeling Miserable

Hector was unable to giggle or chuckle at a single snap. He was too upset about his father's girlfriend. He had hoped it would be possible for his mother and father to get back together.

"This is horrible!" Hector said to Ann. "This is terrible! I feel so miserable. The sensible thing is for my mother and father to stay married and to live together. Life would be so simple if my father would move back into our house. Am I asking for the impossible?"

"Maybe your parents are not able to live together," said Ann. "Living together may just not be possible for them. Your mother is unable to forget the beatings he used to give her, so she does not want him back. Your father is lonely, so he found a new girlfriend. Your parents will probably get a divorce."

Hector began to shake. His hands began to tremble. He banged his fist on a marble table and cried out, "I don't want my parents to get a divorce! I want us to stay together as a family!"

"Don't let the struggle between your parents cripple you," said Ann. "It's not your battle. Changing the situation may not be possible. You should accept the bad things you cannot change, and enjoy the good things in life.

"Isn't it incredible that your father came out of prison just in time to save your life and Kate's! You should be glad just to be alive! Be thankful that your father has not returned to a life of crime, and he is staying out of trouble. At least you can see your father. Look at Jack. His father died from smoking cigarettes. He will never see him again! There will always be bad things in life. You have to enjoy the good."

Hector and Ann were sitting in the middle of the living room couch. Hector cuddled up next to Ann as she hugged him and rocked him like a baby in a cradle. Ann knew just how to handle Hector when he was in a bad mood. After a while, she began to tickle him on his side. Hector began to giggle. Then he sat up and said, "You are right, Ann. I don't want the battle between my parents to cripple me. I cannot control their life. I can only control my life — and I am going to make my life a good life! I don't want to follow my father's example. I want to do good things in my life, and not end up in jail! I want to help myself and to be good to other people. When I get married, I hope to stay with my wife for life."

Hector looked at Ann. There was a sparkle in Hector's eye, and a twinkle in Ann's. Ann thought the dimple on Hector's cheek was cute. Hector thought the freckles on Ann's nose were adorable. Hector and Ann kissed a very long and tender kiss. "I hope we are still together when I'm old enough to get married," said Hector. I would love to spend my life with you."

The kids at the party were looking at Hector and Ann. Some of them started to giggle. "OK lovebirds," said Kate. "I am sorry to bust your bubble. You two look so comfortable snuggling up together, and I know you are both so lovable and kissable, but it's time to return to the snapping contest."

Hector grabbed an apple, and Ann took a sample of maple candy from a dish.

Nat took out a bugle and blew on the horn. "Round three of the snapping contest," he said. "Whose turn is it?"

"Mine," said Bill. "I'm going to dazzle you with this snap. It's a riddle. What's that pimple on top of your neck? ... Sorry! It's your head!"

"No dazzle to that one!" said Nat. "Mike's turn."

"Your father is so stupid," said Mike, "he put a lit candle into the oven to see if the gas was on."

"A little better," said Kate, "but I don't want to settle for a little better. How about a really good snap!"

"Your sister is so skinny," said Tim, "she puts a saddle on her poodle and rides the dog to school."

"When your brother starts to sniffle," said Ann, "he blows his nose into a bottle of pickle juice. Then he adds apple juice. When it rains or drizzles, he adds rainwater from a puddle. He puts it all in a bottle with a label that says mouth wash. Your family loves to gargle with it. That's why all the members of your family have the same horrible breath."

"Ann really dazzled us with that one," said Nat. "Jill, can you top that one?"

"I like the title of your new book," said Jill. "It's called, *Everything I Know*. It's one page long, and the page has only one word — Duh!"

"That was terrible," said Kate, "but cheer up. It's in the running for the dumbest snap trophy."

"My turn," said Hector. "I just read a book about your family. The title is *The Jungle Book*."

"I go," said Jack. "Your head is so round, the school basketball team uses it to practice their dribble."

"Here is my snap," said Flame. "I asked your father why he drove his convertible through the car wash with its top down. 'Not to worry' he said. 'I had my goggles on.'"

"OK," said Kate. "This is the last break for refreshments, and your last chance to sample that incredible ice cream cake with white icing and whipped cream!"

WORD LIST 35 (c=/s/, g=/j/)
1. 'g'=/j/ and 'c'=/s/, when followed by 'e', 'i', or 'y'.
2. The sound /j/ at the end of a word is spelled 'ge'.

can	ace	gas	edge
cop	race	God	pledge
cup	face	gum	judge
city	place	gi ant	fudge
cy cle	space	gym	smudge
cen ter	grace	gen tle	grudge
ice	ice	magic	dodge
pen cil	nice	stin gy	bulge
gro cer y	price	di gest	orange
bi cy cle	rice	sponge	age
suc ceed	mice	huge	cage
ex cept	twice	cross	rage
ex cited	ad vice	clogs	stage
ex cite ment	prac tice	chew ing	change
ac ci dent	dance	bel ly	charge
ce ment	chance	pen al ty	large
cele brate	trance	clean ing	strange
cars	fence	ban dage	ar range
icing	force	can dles	re ar range
ex cel lent	racing		

For Reading Only

straight
sponge
piece
toss
trophies

Word List 35   (g=/j/, c=/s/)

A Chance at Magic

"Do we have any more of that incredible ice cream cake with white icing and whipped cream!" asked Bill. "I want a big piece! Don't be stingy. "

"This is an apartment, not a grocery store," said Jill. "We're all out of ice cream cake. I can give you a slice of orange sponge cake with hot fudge and a cup of soda. Be careful not to smudge any of the fudge on the couch. Jack's mother will kill him if you mess up her couch."

Big Bill sat on the edge of the couch, taking care not to spill any of the orange sponge cake with fudge.

"Didn't you have ice cream cake with fudge, nuts, and whipped cream twice already?" Jack asked. "How can you digest all that food? How can you arrange all that food on one plate. If you force too much food into your belly, you are going to pass gas. You keep eating like that, and you are going to be huge. Your shirt is already an extra extra large. Your belly is already beginning to bulge. I heard you went to the Giant Clothing Store with your girlfriend, but they wouldn't let you in. They said there was not enough space in the place for the two of you at the same time."

"Excellent snap!" said Kim. "Too bad you didn't save it for the contest. Before we started this party, everyone made a pledge not to snap, except on their turn and not at any of *us*. Snapping like that on Bill was not nice, and now you have to pay the price. We are going to charge you with a penalty. When your chance to snap comes up, we are going to skip your turn. Take my advice, if you don't want your friends to have a grudge against you, save your snaps for the contest. It's a cycle. You snap on kids, and kids snap back on you, and everyone ends up mad. As God is my judge, If you don't change, you won't have any friends! You cannot succeed in life if you go around hurting people's feelings all the time. Why don't you act your age!"

"Sorry," said Jack, who was chewing some gum. "Give me a chance! I was only kidding!"

"Well, I didn't get the joke!" said Bill. "I am going to make a pledge to you. If you snap on me like that one more time, I am going to sit on your ugly face! Maybe you won't look so strange after I rearrange your face!"

"Cool it," said Nat. "Everyone is going to get excited. We don't want anyone getting into a rage. Bill, it's your turn. How about an ugly snap."

"OK," said Bill looking straight at Jack. "You're so ugly, when you were born a cop put you in a cage with some mice. Your face is so strange that whenever you cross the street in the center of the city, cars get into an accident."

"My turn," said Mike. "You are so skinny, we could use your head as a pencil."

"You have no grace," said Tim, holding his hands out as if he were sleep walking. "You dance like you are in a trance."

"You and your friend were on a bicycle," said Ann. "Your friend wanted to race you to the fence. You're so stupid, you didn't slow down before you got to the fence. Your bicycle hit the fence, and you went flying into the air and landed on the cement. You celebrated all the way to the hospital, because you won the race. You had a bandage all over your head and face, but you were excited, because you thought you were an ace at bicycle racing."

"My turn," said Jill. "You are so dull that for excitement you pretend it's your wedding day and toss rice into the air, and then you spend the rest of the day cleaning up the rice."

"Your head is so round," said Flame, "they use it in gym to practice playing dodge ball."

"It's my chance to snap," said Jack.

"Sorry," said Kate. "You lost your chance on the snapping stage when you snapped on Mike during snack break."

"I'll take Jack's turn," said Jill. "Your father's ears are so dirty, he can pull out enough wax to make candles."

"My turn," said Hector. "Your father is so dirty, he lost ten pounds by taking a shower. They don't let him go to the gym any more, because every time he takes a shower, he clogs up the drain."

"The contest is over," said Nat. "Time for the trophies! Kate, tell us who won."

Kate said, "The trophy for the dumbest snap goes to Bill for: *when you were born you looked like a cow. When the doctor slapped you on the butt, you said 'Moo!'*"

"The trophy for the best snap goes to Hector," said Nat. "The best snap is: *Your father is so cheap, for his honeymoon, he took your mother on a cruise — in a bathtub*".

"That was a great party!" said Jill.

"Yes," said Kate. "It was like magic. Everyone had a chance to snap, and a lot of the snaps were not too gentle, but nobody got mad. Nobody got into a rage."

"Maybe we're finally growing up," said Hector.

WORD LIST 36 (-ous, -ture, ci-, ti-, -sion)

1. 'ous' = /us/ (as in famous).
2. '-ture' = /chure/, (as in picture).
3. '-sion' = /shun/ (as in mansion) or /zhun/ (as in vision).
4. 'ci' and 'ti' = /sh/ as in (special, vicious, patient, nation).

ner vous	pic ture	man sion	pa tient
fa mous	fu ture	pas sion	an cient
fab u lous	na ture	mis sion	cau tious
gen er ous	lec ture	per mis sion	vi cious
hu mor ous	cap ture	ad mis sion	de licious
re dic u lous	fur ni ture	com pas sion	su per sti tious
poi son ous	temper a ture	vi sion	so cial
e norm ous ly	ad ven ture	de ci sion	of fi cial
tre men dous ly	climb ing	di vi sion	spe cial
dan ger ous	prom ised	tel e vi sion	ra cial
hap py	peace	ex pe di tion	ma gi cian
hoping	nevertheless	ses sions	e lec trician

For Reading Only
Sometimes "gh" = /f/

laugh
laughing
tough
jealous
friendship
neither

WORD LIST 36 suffixes: ous, ture; ci and ti = /sh/, -sion)

Especially for You

"We have had a tremendously interesting year together," said Nat. "Some of us will be going away for the summer. I don't want to be superstitious, but I started the year singing a rap song. I would like to finish the year with another rap song. I hope this one is better than the first one. Ann does not have to give me a kiss this time, if my rap song is a good one."

"I can tap my lip to the rap," said Tim.

"And I can clap to the rap," said Ann. "and if it's a good rap song, I will give Nat a *kiss*."

Nat said, "I am the man! I can rap! I am a champ at rap! I can rap for a kiss!"

Hector and Kate looked at Nat and then began to laugh. All the kids were cracking up. They could not stop laughing.

"Remember when Hector gave Nat a fat lip because Nat wanted Ann to kiss him for rap song?" said Tim.

"Yes," said Ann. "And it was all your fault, Tim, because you had a big trap. You went around saying *he said she said* until Hector got mad at Nat."

"I think I have come a long way," said Hector. "I won't fall for that *he said she said* stuff, now. I won't be jealous just because Ann promised Nat a kiss for a rap song. Let's go Nat. Let's hear your rap."

"I am the man!" said Nat. "I can rap! I am a champ at rap! I can rap for a kiss! Here is a special rap for a special group of kids."

Thank you for permission to talk about my vision
Of how to stick together without fighting or division.
If you want to get along, just listen to my song,
Because peace is my passion, and friendship is my mission.

Now, don't get nervous, it's really not ridiculous,
If someone snaps at you, just look at him as humorous,
If you don't think it's funny, you can always walk away,
Because fighting is so poisonous, and peace is just so fabulous.

 Now, Hector took Ann on a dangerous adventure,
They got lost in a cave where there wasn't any furniture,
Hector said he's sorry, which was such a big admission,
He just wasn't cautious on this climbing expedition.

The cave was so dark that they thought they lost their vision,
Going left or going right was such a very tough decision.
Now, Ann is not a magician, and Hector is not an electrician,
But Ann had a match, and Hector lit it with permission.

Hector ate Pete's beans; they were really so delicious,
But when Pete boxed Hector's ears, it was really very vicious,

But Hector kept his cool, and he didn't raise the temperature,
Keep the rule for keeping cool, and you'll live to see the future.

Thanks for listening to my lecture,
You have been so very patient
I hope you all have got the picture,
Of how to live until you're ancient.

Now, we've had a lot of fun, and we've all been very social,
School is almost over, and it soon will be official,
But before I say goodbye, there's one more thing for us to capture,
Have compassion on each other,
Live together with your brother,
Love your father and your mother,
Make your life a great adventure,
And live in harmony with nature.

    Ann walked over to Nat and gave him a quick kiss on the cheek. "Nat," said Ann "You are a champ at rap! Some day you'll be famous and live in a big mansion. Maybe, we will see you on television"
    Hector did not get jealous this time, and neither did Kate. As Kate walked out with Nat, she was hoping that her father would some day get over his racial attitude. Nevertheless, Kate and Nat were happy together.
    "Thanks for the delicious food," Hector said to Jack. "It was really very generous of you." That was the first time Hector could remember ever saying something nice to Jack.

    The sun was setting, as Hector and Ann walked hand in hand out of Jack's apartment, Hector was thinking about his father. Hector knew that his father and mother were not getting back together, but he also knew he could see his father on weekends. Hector knew one other thing. He could always depend on Ann to stick by him. Hector felt enormously happy. He was even at peace with Jack. He knew that Jack's snaps would never get him to lose his cool again. Hector felt at peace with the world for the first time in his life.

Made in United States
North Haven, CT
24 July 2023